TYRANTS of & TELLERS

STAND
TALL
BUILD
A MASCULINE CULTURE
WIN
THE WAR ON MEN

SONNY ARVADO

www.strengthbysonny.com

Formatting provided by **Archangel Ink**

ISBN-13: 978-1-9744-7314-4

DEDICATION

For Tigger ☺

CONTENTS

Introduction 1

Part I: Culture & Chaos **5**

Chapter 1: "Culture is everything and everything is culture." 7

Chapter 2: Boiling frogs, tied up elephants, and why are lobsters so damn expensive? 11

Chapter 3: Why is there a war on men? 17

Chapter 4: "From Chuck to Cuck"- How Hollywood Destroys Masculinity via Mass Scale Psyops 27

Chapter 5: The Weaponization of Sex 43

Chapter 6: Portrait of the Modern Man 49

Part II: Of Tyrants & Tellers **53**

Chapter 7: "Civilizations and the individual are one and the same." 55

Chapter 8: "Everything flows from health and physical fitness." 63

Chapter 9: The *Of Tyrants & Tellers* Weighlifting Program aka "Basic Cable" 67

Chapter 10: This is Conor McGregor's secret to dominating fights. 109

Chapter 11: "Master of Sex"- How to Defeat the Pornography Psyop Once and For All 129

Chapter 12: The Age of Heroes 133

One Small Request **135**

About the Author **137**

EndNotes **139**

INTRODUCTION

"Build the brand" said the man with the plan

For the man with the plan is the one who can

And The One who can will escape the cellars

Welcome to the world Of Tyrants & Tellers."

Of Tyrants & Tellers: Stand Tall. Build a Masculine Culture. Win the War on Men. Goddamn I fucking love it! You know I came up with this title nearly two years ago. I was in my apartment in Las Vegas. What exactly was I doing? I was laying on my couch staring up at the ceiling. A part of me was lost and searching for that next big move or that next big idea. Or it could have simply been one of those instances where it was just me and my thoughts. Those brief moments of solitude are important because that's when you get down to good old-fashioned thinking.

I started thinking about culture. I started to think about *my* culture. Was it where it needed to be? No, there were several tweaks I needed to make to get back on track and ultimately reach that next level, both as a writer and as a person.[1] Most importantly, I started thinking about *the culture,* specifically the culture of the West. In my experience, cultures function in a zero-sum game. Cultures can be positive, winning cultures that value infrastructure and the betterment of all people involved. They can also be losing cultures characterized by chaos and degeneracy...

Of Tyrants and Tellers is the culmination of nearly two years of obsession with this culture in the West, specifically with the role of men. My side of the Internet is constantly pointing out (and downright complaining) that "the system is rigged against men." Yes, we can all agree that this is indeed the case. But cookie cutter statements like this are unrefined and barely scratch the surface. More importantly, they give no hope for the future.

This work is a complete look at mankind and its relation to culture through the lens of past, present, and depending on YOU, a very bright future. Now you may be wondering why this book focuses solely on men and how they relate to modern-day culture. My answer is twofold. First, this side of the Internet is an area I fell into by chance nearly four years ago when I started my website, strengthbysonny.com. My work in the areas of fitness, professional networking, and personal brand building have enabled me to grow into a trusted figure in the study of masculinity. Second, and more importantly, I see what has happened to Western civilization and I see the path we are heading down. The culture's all-out war on mankind, namely the virtues of strength and masculinity, will ultimately lead to the collapse of the West.

Civilization has always rested on the shoulders of strong, masculine men who build infrastructure and drive the culture forward. Think of any great cultural or architectural accomplishment that has withstood the test of time. Athenian democracy. The Great Wall of China. The Hoover Dam. These were built by men. Unfortunately, since the second half of the twentieth-century, we have seen a *de-evolution* of culture. A culture that once valued strength and masculinity has gotten to the point where these important virtues are now vilified.

This systemic collapse will be discussed at great length in the first part of this work.

The second part of this work is the answer for all men. Its purpose is not to tell you "how to be a man," nor is it meant to help you find your "life's purpose." These are answers you will arrive at on your own when you are ready. It is about using the tools outlined for you to build your own culture, one built upon a foundation of strength and masculinity. By the time you have finished this work, you will have the long-term game plan to make your personal brand a respectable one that you are proud of. As an individual, you absolutely matter to the future of mankind. Always remember that. Now let's bring back strength once and for all!

PART I

CULTURE & CHAOS

Chapter 1:
"CULTURE IS EVERYTHING AND EVERYTHING IS CULTURE."

A man's brand is rooted in his culture. Remember these words because they will be hammered into your head throughout this work: Culture is everything and everything is culture. It all matters. Everything. Everything and anything. Your culture is the reason why you are *who you are right now*. Your culture is the reason why you are *where you are right now*. Every single event and experience leading up to you reading this work is the result of your culture. I guess my questions for you now are: Are you content with your culture? Are you even aware of your culture? Since you are reading this work, chances are you are not quite content with your culture. Either that, or perhaps you're simply a go-getter who is always looking for the next thing to improve upon. I am also willing to bet that it's very likely that you have not taken the time to truly assess your culture.

But let's stick to this notion of culture, in particular the *when* and the *who*. When does your culture begin to take shape? I would argue that your culture begins when you are born. In fact, one could make the argument that your culture begins before birth, as several studies indicate the benefits of parents reading to their unborn babies while still in the womb.[2] Yes, this represents the beginning of culture, and a positive one at that. If only more parents did this! Either way, I think we can all agree that your culture begins to take form at a very early age.

That leaves us with the question of who is responsible for your culture. As you get older, you take on greater responsibility for your culture, but in reality, external influences play a huge role in the development of your culture. Your parents play perhaps the biggest role in the development of your culture. In fact, a growing number of incompetent parents, such as those with helicopter parenting tendencies, are destroying the culture of boys. This ultimately hinders their chances of ever becoming men.[3] For all intents and purposes, your culture is the product of all external factors that influence your way of life. Your culture is the music you listen to; the way you dress so that you "fit in" with the cool kids; the viral memes and jokes you see on social media; and the people you interact with, both face to face and virtually, throughout your life. Most importantly, the majority of your culture is the product of the messages repeatedly hammered into your consciousness by the various forms of media and the *shadow oligarchs* who control it.

So how much of your culture are you truly responsible for? Or better yet, how much of your culture do you *own*? You might argue that you have complete control and ownership of your culture. That's an optimistic way of looking at things. But is it reality? Not really. This should be the cause of concern. You have grown up in a world where you have very little control over the development of your personal culture. You don't own it. It owns you and shapes you based purely off of circumstances. If you were lucky, you grew up under the guidance of a strong father figure who conditioned you to be a strong, masculine figure yourself. That used to be the norm, but today that is a far reaching best case scenario that a continually shrinking population of young men benefit from. Most young men are not lucky because their entire culture and masculine identity is left up to a combination of single mother households and mainstream pop culture.

If a man's brand is rooted in his culture, what does this say about *the brand* today, both for the individual and the masses? The masses depend upon the individual because the masses are comprised of individuals. Most men today are soft, effeminate, beta male pussies. And it is because of *the culture*. The media's all-out war on masculinity and vilification of anything resembling a masculine culture will be the end of Western civilization as we know it. All you have to do is open your eyes and take a look around in any public space in any city. Everywhere you look the men are emasculated pansies. They have zero masculine identity and half of them you cannot even tell if they are men or women. Today, the average Western male looks, talks, and conducts himself more like a woman than a man. Is this progress? Is this the future you want to be a part of, or worse, *fit in* with? As will be illustrated in the ensuing chapters, this is no accident but rather the result of a strategically implemented process of chemical and cultural castration that has transpired since the mid-twentieth century.

Chapter 2:
BOILING FROGS, TIED UP ELEPHANTS, AND WHY ARE LOBSTERS SO DAMN EXPENSIVE?

While we're on the topic of culture, let's talk about change, specifically changing culture. We have already argued that mankind has changed for the worse as a result of cultural degeneracy. But how does this happen? How does culture *change*? Is this a rapid process that takes place overnight or is this a slow, drawn out process? To answer this question, I am going to explain it through the use of three animals as analogies. Regular readers of *Strength By Sonny* are already familiar with the first two analogies.[4] The third analogy takes a more holistic look into a cultural phenomenon and will lead us directly into our discussion on the war on men.

BOILING FROGS

Have you ever heard of the boiling frog analogy? If not, then it goes something like this: Supposedly, if you put a frog in a boiling pot of water, the frog will immediately sense the heat and jump out. However, if you put a frog in a pot of water at room temperature and slowly turn up the heat to boil, the frog will die. We are all frogs at some point because someone somewhere is slowly turning up the heat on us. Are we going to jump out in time? This is culture.

TIED UP ELEPHANTS

In the beginning of his iconic book, *Shadow Men: An Encyclopedia of Mind Control,* Dr. Anthony Napoleon actually begins his first chapter on the mind by discussing how zookeepers keep big, powerful adult elephants captive with nothing more than small rope tied around one of the elephant's legs.[5] How do they do it? A massive elephant has the ability to uproot trees. A small piece of rope should be nothing. The answer lies with mind control, or should we say, culture control, that starts at a very early age. When a baby elephant is held in captivity, he is initially chained by the ankle. He tries to escape but the chain digs into his flesh causing immense physical and emotional pain. His repeated attempts are futile. Eventually, the baby elephant succumbs to defeat and gives up trying to escape. The chain is eventually replaced with a rope. Although the elephant grows up to be a big, powerful creature, he never tries to escape. Why? The elephant recalls the painful memories of the past. He remembers all of the times his failure was met with excruciating pain. He remains captive forever. This is culture.

WHY ARE LOBSTERS SO DAMN EXPENSIVE?

Have you ever gone to a nice restaurant and looked to see what the most expensive thing on the menu was? What was it? More times than not, the most expensive thing on the menu is either the surf n' turf or something else involving lobster. But why? What's so special about lobster? Does it taste better than all other foods? Does it hold more nutritional value than other foods? Does it fill you up? What is it?

The answer is… NOTHING. There is nothing special about lobster. It doesn't taste better than other foods. In fact, one could argue that it is an inferior crustacean to crab and shrimp in every way. And there are plenty of other forms of seafood that hold way more nutritional value than lobster. It doesn't even fill you up. No matter how much lobster you eat, you are often left hungry. This is actually how seafood joints get you to buy more food. No, the price of lobster and the status associated with eating it is an artificially created social construct.

To this day, many fishermen still refer to lobsters as the "cockroaches of the sea." They are bottom dwellers. In fact, back when the Europeans were first settling the Americas, lobsters were treated as such by all peoples. The Europeans saw lobsters as bugs and mostly regarded them as unfit for consumption. There was social stigma associated with eating lobster because it was considered low class. Regular folks would only resort to eating it when they were on the brink of starvation. In fact, lobsters were considered such low class that they were fed almost exclusively to slaves and prisoners. Even the Native Americans saw little nutritional value in lobsters, choosing instead to use them primarily as fertilizer for crops.[6] So why are lobsters so damn expensive? The answer is pure, artificially created culture. Somewhere along the way, restaurateurs slowly but surely decided to artificially attach value to an animal that inherently has very little. Talk about a racket!

THE CULTURAL VALUE OF MEN

One final thought to dwell on for this section is the *actual value* versus the *culturally perceived value* of men. How do they compare, or better yet, how have they each changed over time? Without a doubt, the actual value of men has taken a hit, mainly as a result of chemical warfare via the chemicals in food, water, and air pollution. Men have lower testosterone now more than ever and as a result, this has created a generation of men who are softer, both physically and mentally weaker, and very much incompetent when it comes to doing physical labor. That being said, men still hold an advantage over women when it comes to pure drive and ability to get things done. Though it appears that gap is closing quickly.

Now how does this relate to the culturally perceived value of men today? It turns out they are not related at all because the culture has been *engineered* in a way that has betrayed men. Everywhere you look, men and anything associated with masculinity, is routinely vilified to the point of mass hysteria. This mass hysteria, this complete and utter pussification of the West, has infiltrated every single aspect of the culture. This even includes the education system. In recent years, college campuses have ramped up their efforts to become nothing more than liberal brainwashing factories, offering little educational value but plenty of opportunities to culturally attack masculinity. Even prestigious educational institutions, such as Duke University, have resorted to creating "safe spaces" for men to "deconstruct their toxic masculinity."[7]

On the surface, each cultural example seems small and harmless. However, because these examples are seemingly infinite in number and are repeatedly hammered into mass consciousness, they are crystallized into mainstream belief. Some of these include:

"Men are below women."

"It's a bad to be a *manly* man."

"Masculinity is *toxic*."

But now the gig is up. The masses are waking up and realizing that civilization depends on strong, masculine men who will drive it forward. You are at the forefront of this.

Chapter 3:
WHY IS THERE A WAR ON MEN?

It's not a question of whether or not there is a war on men. The answer is obvious. There absolutely is a war on men. Believe it or not, there is also a war on women, but that's a story for another day. However, we will make reference to it later in this chapter. Both wars are intertwined and the interesting thing to note is that this gradual warfare that is being waged on both sexes entails the same two-front attack: chemical and cultural warfare.

CHEMICAL WARFARE

Let's discuss the chemical aspect of the war on men because it is the most direct, and arguably, most effective form of warfare. To be honest, there really isn't a whole lot to say regarding chemical warfare because as with the culture war, the chemical war is everywhere. The difference is that with the culture war, there are viable solutions and victory is attainable by you. This is what the entirety of Part II is dedicated to. You will be taking ownership of your culture.

However, the chemical war is a far more uphill battle. Many enlightened minds would argue that it is nearly impossible to win. I would have to agree. If you live in or near any major metropolis in the West, you have been impacted by chemical warfare. The food you eat, the water you drink, the air you breathe, and the products you consume have all been laced with endocrine disrupting chemicals. Check out the label on any food you consume. Chances are it says: "Contains Soy" in small letters at the bottom. Soy holds little nutritional value and is downright poisonous to both the male and female endocrine systems. Some of the side effects of long-term soy consumption for men include: increase in estrogen levels, decreased libido, and lowered sperm count.[8] Clearly, soy is a masculinity destroyer. However, that doesn't stop the mainstream media, such as *The Huffington Post*, from pumping out articles on the virtues of soy and its health benefits for men.[9] Keep in mind, this is the same media at the forefront of the cultural war being waged on men.

The same goes for the water you drink. As with the food you eat, the water you have been drinking since birth is also polluted with endocrine disrupting chemicals, namely fluoride. Fluoride is touted as an essential nutrient, particularly as it relates to overall tooth health and the prevention of tooth decay. This is why all the toothpaste you see in stores reads: "Contains Fluoride." This is a scam. In fact, from 1986 to 1987, the National Institute of Dental Research (NIDR) conducted its largest survey ever where they examined the teeth of 39,207 schoolchildren from 84 communities across the country, including communities that fluoridated their water and communities that did not.[10] The results indicated that the difference in tooth decay between communities with fluoridated and non-fluoridated water was so insignificant to the point of putting claims of fluoride's role in having any impact in reducing tooth decay into serious doubt.[11]

Not only does water fluoridation have zero medical benefits, it actually poses many serious health risks so much so that 97% of Europe has banned the practice of fluoridating the water. Some of the more serious side effects from long-term consumption of fluoridated water can include: weakened skeletal muscle, lowered sperm count, and negative cognitive effects. Furthermore, from a purely hormonal standpoint one study conducted in China specifically researched the endocrine disturbing effect of fluoride, with a focus on districts with higher concentrations of fluoride versus districts that contained little to no concentrations of fluoride. This study concluded that the serum level of testosterone for men in the fluoridated districts were significantly lower than the levels of men in non-fluoridated districts. Furthermore, the study also concluded that the serum level of testosterone for women in the fluoridated districts was significantly higher than that of women in non-fluoridated districts. So ultimately, this study indicated that elevated levels of fluoride in the environment (water, food, and soil) significantly decreased serum levels of testosterone for men and significantly increased them for women.[12] This is the exact opposite of what you would want for either men or women!

Look, let's be honest here. When it comes to the chemical war being waged on the masses, the majority of people are fucked. Most of the damage has already been done during the early years of development. By the time people wake up and realize just how harmful these chemicals and pollutants really are its way too late to naturally combat this and reverse the damage. This brings me to the best solution I have for men.

HOW TO FIGHT BACK AGAINST ALL OUT CHEMICAL WARFARE

There are several ways to avoid this chemical onslaught on the male endocrine system, but most of them are either dependent on pure luck or widely impractical. Pay close attention to the last one.

1) Be born to parents who grew up in the wilderness or far away from developed cities.

2) Be born in the wilderness, live there forever, and be completely self-sufficient; only consume food and water from the wild.

3) Luck out in the genetic lottery.

4) Testosterone Replacement Therapy - Take matters into your own hands.

Numbers 1 through 3 are a pipe dream for most. Number 4 is the most practical solution and most importantly, a direct solution to the chemical war being waged on men. You take matters into your own hands. If you grew up in the West and numbers 1-3 do not apply to you, it's almost a guarantee that you have low testosterone. While I am well-versed enough on the topic of testosterone and testosterone replacement therapy (TRT) to educate the uninitiated, I will leave that discussion for another time. The purpose of this work is to focus primarily on the cultural war being waged on men. Significant time spent on anything else would take away from this purpose.

For all answers pertaining to testosterone and testosterone replacement therapy, check out Jay Campbell's book, *The Definitive Testosterone Replacement Therapy MANual*. He has nearly 20 years of experience in that realm and his information will explain things far more in-depth than I ever could. His website trtrevolution.com also contains a lot of helpful information on this as well.

CULTURAL WARFARE

This brings us to the culture war and ultimately, the why. Why *exactly* is there a war on men? Is it just to spite men? Is it because someone, somewhere wants to level the playing field? After all, men have been the movers and shakers since the dawn of time. Maybe the *shadow oligarchs* simply want to give other people a shot...

No, if you dig deep enough you will find that the answer is darker and far more wide-reaching than you could possibly imagine. But I'm going to hit you with it right now. The plain and simple truth is that most men are uninformed and downright disillusioned when it comes to the war on men. Well, let's take a step back for a minute. Most men have no idea that there is even a war on men. They just don't. They simply go about their normal routines and accept the reality of the world with which they are presented. Then you have the men who know something is up but they just can't quite put their finger on it. Many of them take on a losing victim mentality, governed by a "You can't be a man these days!" mantra. They believe war is being waged on men just to "get back at men" or level the playing field. But these answers are dead wrong. The truth is that there is nothing personal about this war. It's business. The war on men is cold business that is conducted with one big agenda in mind.

Think about this for a minute. There are many different agendas that the mainstream media continues to hammer into mass consciousness. You certainly don't have to read this work to know that. You don't have to be anywhere close to being an enlightened individual to see through the bullshit that is shoved down the masses' throats 24/7. Even the average mouth-breather glued to their smartphone can distinguish certain messages that are continuously promoted. Some of the most prominent ones include: feminism, globalism, the gay agenda, false rape culture, destruction of the family unit, and the all-out assault on traditional values.

However, these are simply a means to an end. When you put all of the pieces together you will realize that the ultimate goal, the true agenda of the secret elite, is: *depopulation.*[13] The *shadow oligarchs,* the puppet masters behind the scenes, the true movers and shakers of the world, are working toward making the world a *smaller* place. Now why are they doing this? They are doing this because the world is getting too big. There are too many people on the planet. This is a problem for the *masters* because the more people there are, the more difficult it becomes to control them. An already massive population, that continues to grow, increases the risk of exhausting the planet's resources. Such a population also brings with it a growing subset of critical thinkers who have woken up and understand what's really going on. On top of that, the power of the Internet will only unify the opposition. Overall, this potential loss of control presents major issues and is a nightmare from a management standpoint. Thus, pulling out all the stops to shrink the global population by means of both chemical and cultural warfare, in a gradual undetectable process, is the only logical conclusion.

But don't just take my word for it. You don't even have to search long and hard for answers. Just listen to what the elites have to say! They flat out admit it![14]

"A total world population of 250-300 million people, a 95% decline from present levels, would be ideal." – CNN Founder Ted Turner

"The negative impact of population growth on all of our planetary ecosystems is becoming appallingly evident." – David Rockefeller

"We humans have become a disease, the Humanpox."
– David Foreman, Co-founder of Earth First

"The world today has 6.8 billion people. That's heading up to about nine billion. Now if we do a really great job on new vaccines, health care, reproductive health services, we could lower that by perhaps 10 or 15 percent." – Microsoft Founder Bill Gates

"A program of sterilizing women after their second or third child, despite the relatively greater difficulty of the operation than vasectomy, might be easier to implement than trying to sterilize men." – John P. Holdren, President Obama's primary science adviser

"In order to stabilize world population, we must eliminate 350,000 people per day." – Jacques Cousteau

One last quote that you may find of interest comes from the Georgia Guidestones, a granite monument anonymously constructed in 1980 that contains a set of 10 guidelines inscribed on it. These guidelines are meant to govern humanity. The first guideline states: "Maintain humanity under 500,000,000 in perpetual balance with nature."

The depopulation agenda is not a conspiracy. It's not fantasy. It's not wishful thinking. It's a known reality. The evidence is clear, both chemically and culturally. The elites are on record admitting it out in the open. It simply goes over everyone's heads because they are too busy staring at their screens. This leaves the *how*. How are they going to accomplish this? Better yet, how are they *already* accomplishing this?

ANDROGYNY

I wasn't joking when I said that there was a war on women as well. When you consider the world and the mass propaganda that governs its people in terms of one, big depopulation agenda, this starts to make sense. Imagine if you were a member of the secret elite who wanted to shrink down the population of the world in order to make it more *manageable*. How would you do it?

All out physical warfare or blatant extermination of mass populations wouldn't do the trick. First, it would be too costly and getting the resources required to pull off such an operation would be quite the challenge. Second, it would be way too obvious. Yes, the masses are largely brainwashed idiots but they are not that dumb. Even though mass consciousness has been weathered down to a nub, we are not robots just yet. We are not at a point where the people would accept massive worldwide extermination without putting up a fight. Instead, the closest thing to extermination you could probably get away with is subtle, all-encompassing chemical warfare that impacts both sexes on a daily basis. As stated earlier, this is exactly what has been transpiring.

What else might work? Well, think about it from the other side of the spectrum. How do you *increase* the population? The population increases when there is an *increase* in procreation between men and women. An increase in birthrate is one of the tell-tale signs of a society with healthy, optimized hormones, or a high testosterone civilization.[15] This is exactly what happened in the United States during the post-World War II years, which many consider to be the Golden Age of America. The economic boom that America experienced enabled the creation of physical infrastructure and more importantly, social infrastructure. The U.S. was fresh off of a big time victory in World War II and there were plenty of jobs and money to go around. So people started creating infrastructure by having children and keeping those families intact. The American Dream, the goal of average Americans at this time, was represented by the pursuit of the accumulation of wealth and raising families. Everyone knew their place. The men were strong, masculine providers for the family. The women were feminine homemakers who took care of the home and raised the children. As a member of the secret elite, this is the worst case scenario because this new wave development of strong, traditional nuclear families would essentially create "islands of power and wealth" outside of your control.[16] No, you could not let that happen. You would do everything within your power to bring this type of infrastructure and self-sufficiency to a screeching halt…

Instead, you would do everything within your power to destroy the very idea of forming families. How would you do this? You would embark on a slow but steady social engineering project in which you turn the world upside down. You would discourage heterosexual relations between men and women in every possible way. You would vilify it and even go so far as to make people fearful of it.[17] In place, you would heavily promote and glorify homosexuality. You would wage an all-out war on traditional gender roles. Instead, you would promote a complete reversal of gender roles by making the men more feminine and the women more masculine. Sound familiar? It should, because this is the reality you see every single day. This goal of combining male and female sexual characteristics and traits into one gender, or androgyny, is the means by which they are subtly "trimming the fat." A small, androgynous population is ideal for the masters because this is a dream come true for management purposes.

No Men = No Fight = Easy Control

Chapter 4:
"FROM CHUCK TO CUCK"- HOW HOLLYWOOD DESTROYS MASCULINITY VIA MASS SCALE PSYOPS

Let's stick with this concept of androgyny as it is relevant now more than ever. Do any examples come to mind? I've got one. Let's talk about the normalization of transgenderism. This is a hot topic today because it has sparked many debates and is just one of many issues that divides the masses. Those who are infected with the progressive virus will dismiss science by arguing that sex and gender are social constructs.[18] Anybody can be anything! But the cold hard truth is that you can't fight science. Don't take my word for it though. Listen to the true experts. Dr. Paul R. McHugh, the former psychiatrist-in-chief for Johns Hopkins Hospital, and its current Distinguished Service Professor of Psychiatry, shuts the door on this fantasy in stating that sex change is "biologically impossible" and that transgenderism is nothing more than a "mental disorder" that should be treated as such.[19]

However, science and just plain old common sense have no place in Hollywood, because the establishment has been relentless in unleashing their propaganda machines onto the masses. Bruce

Jenner was the puppet they used to promote acceptance of this mental illness. The story of Bruce Jenner's destruction is a tragic one because it exemplifies the destruction of masculine culture at large.[20] For those of you who are unfamiliar with his story, Bruce Jenner was once *the* all-American sports hero, as evidenced by his victory in the decathlon at the 1976 Summer Olympics. He was the poster child for everything a man aspired to be. However, like the boiling frog, Hollywood slowly destroyed him. Once he stepped into the world of entertainment, these *shadow oligarchs* chipped away at his masculinity. Slowly but surely he became more feminine until 2015 when Bruce Jenner officially became a transgender woman named Caitlin Jenner. The transformation was complete. Right on cue, the media hammered this into mainstream consciousness with widespread reporting. Bruce Jenner's transformation and "bravery" dominated the headlines. He/She even received the Arthur Ashe Award for Courage at the 2015 ESPY Awards. However, this process was not unique in any way. In fact, when it comes to cultural influence on a mass scale, it is *the way.*

"IT'S NOT ENTERTAINMENT. IT'S *INFLUENCE.*"

Movies. Television. Music. Sports. Advertising. Social Media. You deal with all of these forms of entertainment on a daily basis. But have you ever asked yourself why these entities exist? Do they exist purely to benefit you, the viewer? Or do they exist simply to make as much money as possible? It turns out, neither answer is correct. Of course, money is always a motivating factor. And in most cases, it's often the biggest factor. But this is different. Your entertainment is icing on the cake, a nice little bonus to keep you distracted. Money, while always great, does little more than move the needle in this case. Besides, the same *shadow oligarchs* who pull all the strings already control all of the money. No, this game has always been about influence.

Neil Gabler's book, *An Empire of the Own: How the Jews Invented Hollywood*, gives great insight into the beginnings of today's modern-day Hollywood. Gabler's work is an interesting read because it explores both the initial thoughts and motivations behind the creation of American entertainment. One of the main points Gabler makes in his work mirrors what was said earlier. Money and entertainment were motivating factors but influence was at the forefront for the founders of Hollywood. The original Jewish studio moguls aspired to create a world that reflected their own views, so they reflected them in their very own films. And in doing so, "the Hollywood Jews created a powerful cluster of images and ideas - so powerful that, in a sense, they colonized the American imagination."[21] It wasn't about entertainment, not even close. It was about claiming ownership of the last frontier on Earth up for grabs, the minds of the masses. The same is true for today.

PSYOPS - A CRASH COURSE ON HOW TO WEAPONIZE IDEAS AND MOLD CULTURE

The long-term destruction of masculinity becomes crystal clear when you break down your thinking of culture in terms of messages and ideas that can be *weaponized*. Yes, ideas can be weaponized over a period of time, in any which way decision makers choose. This process is absolutely scalable to size and, believe it or not, is rooted in tactics originally used by the military and other government agencies.

The term that is used to describe this covert, scalable molding of ideas is referred to as psyops or psychological operations. This is not interpretation or theory. There are entire manuals dedicated to the art of mental warfare. The United States Army has one called, *PSYOP: Military Psychological Operations*. The language of this manual is straight to the point:

Mission

1-5. The mission of PSYOP is to influence the behavior of foreign target audiences (TAs) to support U.S. national objectives. PSYOP accomplish this by conveying selected information and/or advising on actions that influence the emotions, motives, objective reasoning, and ultimately the behavior of foreign audiences. Behavioral change is at the root of the PSYOP mission. Although concerned with the mental processes of the TA, it is the observable modification of TA behavior that determines the mission success of PSYOP. It is this link between influence and behavior that distinguishes PSYOP from other capabilities and activities of information operations (IO) and sets it apart as a unique core capability.[22]

Core Tasks

There are 6 core PSYOP tasks. However, the one on production is most relevant to this work:

Produce. Production is the transformation of approved PSYOP product prototypes into various media forms that are compatible with the way foreign populations are accustomed to receiving information. Some production requirements may be contracted to private industry, while other requirements may be performed by units attached or under the tactical control (TACON) or operational control (OPCON) of PSYOP forces.[23]

The CIA also has its own manual on how to carry out psychological operations. This manual is called the *CIA Manual for Psychological Operations in Guerrilla Warfare*. Its original purpose was to provide

CIA operatives with a step-by-step blueprint for infiltrating and psychologically defeating the Socialist movement of the Nicaraguan Sandinista movement. However, this small 68-page booklet is filled with golden nuggets that can be implemented on a mass scale.

When we think of guerrilla warfare, we often think of surprise military attacks in which an unsuspecting enemy is physically decimated. Right off the bat, this manual states that guerrilla warfare is a political war focused on the "political animal," where the mind is the ultimate goal.

> *"The human being has his most critical point in his mind. Once his mind has been reached, the political animal has been defeated, without necessarily receiving bullets."* [24]

Psychological operations win wars because the target is not territory. When it's obvious that territory is the target, physical conflict is inevitable. This is inefficient warfare because it guarantees casualties and wasted resources for all parties involved. In the wide world of psyops, the target is the minds of the population. Armed Propaganda is the term used to describe every act carried out and every idea that is promoted to a population for the sake of conquest. Sound familiar? Culture is everything and everything is culture. Armed Propaganda is the means by which the few conquer many...

Standard procedure entails the CIA infiltrating a population and molding its culture by sending in Armed Propaganda Teams. These Armed Propaganda Teams are small, under the radar, covert forces. It only takes 6-10 members to carry out an operation. Furthermore, these members are not foreign looking troops decked out in camo. They are trained to blend in. They start small with simple integration into the local population. These operatives go full "native" by working alongside the people, adopting their customs, and becoming contributing members of the community. Cultural influence is not the goal early on. *Building trust* is the name of the game.

Then they get to work. Slowly but surely, the few members of the Armed Propaganda Team start to leak out ideas. It's gradual like a IV drip. They initially focus their efforts on "established citizens" such as doctors, lawyers, businessmen, teachers, etc.[25] The reason why they do this is because these established citizens already have the most respect and status within the population. Winning over the masses and controlling group dynamics becomes that much easier. From there, total control and influence is simply the result of a continuous program of indoctrination. Ideas create dialogue. Dialogues form opinions. Shared opinions become slogans. Slogans become speeches. Speeches draw audiences and movements. Movements become mass scale action.

> *"The human being is made up of a mind and a soul; he acts in accordance with his thoughts and sentiments and responds to stimuli of ideas and emotions."* [26]

One final takeaway to consider is that although this manual is filled with tons of golden nuggets on the snowballing effect of influence, it is this idea of repetition that is emphasized. The first rule of mind control, perhaps the only one that really matters is, repetition. This manual makes it crystal clear that successful psychological warfare is a matter of *constantly hammering away at themes* in order to condition the masses.[27] That's all it takes. Let's take a look at a few examples, a sort of before and after analysis for the various forms of entertainment.

MOVIES

People go to the movies all the time for a variety of reasons. Most people would say they go to the movies for entertainment. You could make a case that people go for *escapism*. In fact, this was the very reason why movie attendances first skyrocketed in America during the 1930s. During this time, America was in the midst of the Great Depression and people needed an outlet to escape reality. Whether or not you think the same logic applies today, there's no doubt that the very act of staring up at the big screen equates to massive influence for whoever owns the screen. Let's take a look at one of the most famous movie characters of all time, James Bond.

James Bond (Sean Connery)

The original James Bond was played by Sean Connery, and if you watch those movies, you can clearly see that he was the gold standard for masculinity. He was always cool, calm, and collected. He was strong, both physically and mentally. He fit the *heroic* archetype by all accounts. Men of all ages looked up to him and wanted to be him. He epitomized everything that a woman would find attractive in a man. For the most part, Hollywood left this character alone. They did not leak any of their masculinity destroying agendas into Connery's portrayal. He was purely James Bond, as originally described by Ian Fleming. This was in the 1960s.

James Bond (Daniel Craig)

Fast forward to the present-day James Bond and you will find a very different character. Daniel Craig's portrayal is far more emotional and you can't help but notice that he always seems to be less in control of the situation compared to the previous Bonds. As a viewer, when you watch this James Bond, you're just not as sure. When you saw Sean Connery on screen, there were no questions. You knew he always had the situation under control. With Daniel Craig, you just never know.

However, the greatest cause for concern is the modern-day James Bond's sexuality. Upon first glance, it's clear that this is the most feminine, metrosexual James Bond to date. In fact, Hollywood takes it a step further and hints at his homosexual tendencies. In *Skyfall*, there is one scene in particular that subtly hints at the homosexual attraction between James Bond and the villain, Raoul Silva. During the initial interrogation, Bond is tied to a chair and Silva initiates homosexual contact. He opens up his shirt, and proceeds to touch all over his body. Silva and Bond playfully smile at one another. Bond even insinuates that this is not the first time another man has done this to him. Audiences laughed in theaters but these types of subtle hints are not thrown in there for the purposes of entertainment but rather *normalization*.

HOLLYWOOD'S DESTRUCTION OF THE BIG SCREEN "HERO"

In a 2015 interview with the *Independent*, Michael Douglas commented on the lack of masculinity in Hollywood, comparing American actors to their global counterparts. "In the US, we have this relatively asexual or unisex area with sensitive young men and we don't have many Channing Tatums or Chris Pratts, while the Aussies do."[28] Mr. Douglas hit the nail on the head and I would actually expand on his point.

In years past, when you saw a male actor in a movie, a part of you actually looked up to him. Whether he was good or bad, you saw him as above you because he embodied a certain heroic quality in one way or another. In his own way, he was strong and masculine. When young men saw *Dirty Harry*, they wanted to be a tough guy like Clint Eastwood. Arnold Schwarzenegger will forever be one of the most iconic actors of all time, because he was the action hero everyone aspired to be. In the *Rocky* movies, Sylvester Stallone inspired young men to give it their all and never give up. Even Michael Douglas, when he played Gordon Gekko in *Wall Street*, left young men in awe when he played one of the most iconic anti-heroes of all time. Whether you loved him or hated him, goddamn you couldn't help but admire him. He was a lean, mean, money making machine who had the world in the palm of his hand. But these movie characters are relics of the past, a past that celebrated the unbreakable alpha male carved out of granite. These figures are extinct in present-day movies.

Watch any movie today and you find a much different man that pops up time and time again. These are not men that audiences look up to. Overall, they are weak. Mentally this goes without saying. They lack certainty, have zero emotional control, and are constantly screwing up. They usually play second fiddle to women as well. Physically, they are *sloppy*. Most of them are estrogenic trainwrecks. There is nothing inspiring about them. No one looks up at a movie screen and wants to be just like Seth Rogen or Jonah Hill. Instead, the masses sit there with their mouths open and laugh. Little do they know, this is all part of Hollywood's strategy to normalize this weak, *sloppy* brand of man.

TELEVISION

Television is another medium that is used as a weapon to slowly mold and normalize culture. This is why it is called *television programming*. This form of media has also been utilized to destroy the public's perception of how a man should look and act.

The Rifleman vs. The Big Bang Theory

These are two different television shows that depict the type of men that are glorified for their respective time periods. Although the men that are portrayed are from two different time periods, they might as well be from two different worlds. Chuck Connors was the actor who played Lucas McCain in *The Rifleman*, a television show that ran from 1958-1963. In this show, Lucas McCain illustrated the heroic masculine ideal. He was the big, strong hero that everyone turned to in times of trouble. He remained confident in all situations.

Compare him to two of the main characters from one of the most popular television shows today, *The Big Bang Theory*. These men have zero masculine qualities that viewers look up to. Everything about them from how they look to how they act is weak and feminine. Sheldon Cooper, played by Jim Parons, is clearly a homosexual. Leonard Hofstadter, portrayed by Johnny Galecki, epitomizes the stereotypical low testosterone beta male who plays second fiddle to his woman.

In addition to the general brand of men, the television has also been an effective tool at destroying the image of the father figure. You don't even have to go as far back as the 1960s to find television shows that idealized strong father figures.

Jack Arnold- *The Wonder Years*

The Wonder Years was one of the most iconic television shows of all time. It told the story of growing up in middle America suburbia when times were simpler. More specifically, the show focuses on Kevin Arnold and his coming of age story from 1968 to 1973, though the show is actually filmed from 1988 to 1993. Kevin's family exemplified the traditional family structure for this time. He had two siblings. His mother was a typical housewife who fulfilled her duties and his father exemplified the model father figure. He was the head of the household. He was strong, masculine and could "fix" just about anything.

Homer Simpson- *The Simpsons*

Around this time (1989), another television show began to air. This show painted a very different picture of the father figure. Over the last thirty years, *The Simpsons* have withstood the test of time and have not only become one of the iconic television shows of all time, but the Simpson family has also come to be considered by many as "America's family." This comes as no surprise, especially when you consider how the father, Homer Simpson, is portrayed. There's nothing masculine about him and he possesses zero admirable traits. In a way, he is America's favorite idiot that the masses can relate to. He's loud, obnoxious, fat, lazy, drinks all the time, and regularly fights with his kids. He's the role model anyone can live up to…

MUSIC- RAP

Music, in particular rap music, has also undergone its own transformation. Now rap music, since its inception, has been nothing more than a form of massive crowd control. Its main purpose is to prevent the building of true infrastructure, both on a personal and societal level. It does this by dumbing down people of all races. It dumbs down blacks by glorifying a life of drugs, violence, and crime that they then aspire to live up to. This is what truly prevents them from advancing in a system that has held them back historically. It dumbs down whites in the same way, thus, destroying infrastructure that has been a historical advantage for them.

However, for the purposes of this discussion let's take a look at how rap music is weaponized against masculinity. Since rap music is relatively young from a cultural standpoint, we find that this process has been rather fast.

50 cent

2003 was an interesting year in the world of rap because this is when 50 Cent first rose to mainstream status. What makes this interesting is that this happened pretty much overnight. He became a mainstream celebrity immediately upon releasing his debut album, *Get Rich or Die Tryin'*, which debuted at #1 and sold 872,000 copies in its first week. The magnitude of 50 Cent's rise to fame has never been matched. This is particularly impressive, considering that this was accomplished before social media came to prominence.

Although 50 Cent's message was pretty much the same as every other "gangsta" rapper, his brand was still one of masculinity. There was nothing feminine about 50 Cent. He fit the big, strong, alpha-male archetype. He dressed and acted like a man who grew up in the ghetto.

Rap Music Today

Fast forward to today and you see a different look being promoted. Big, tough looking dudes wearing baggy clothes and Timberland boots have been replaced with twinks wearing skinny jeans and dresses. Even well-known established rappers like Diddy and Kanye West have been reduced to wearing skirts while up on stage. The general public is dumbfounded by rap's recent fashion trend, but the reason is obvious. Those who control rap behind the scenes are also a part of this widescale effort to normalize the emasculation and feminization of the Western male.

ADVERTISING

Advertising is the same story. Why is it even called advertising? Can we just call it for what it is? Propaganda. In recent years, corporations have also ramped up their efforts to take part in the war on men by devaluing the father. In 2016, Old Navy had a shirt on sale that read "It's Father's Day," but looking at it closely, it said "It's Her Day" in the bold letters. These are the type of subtle attacks that might not seem like much at first glance. However, when every single aspect of the culture is doing this, it becomes clear that there is a war against men.

Absolut Vodka's 2007 global advertising campaign titled, "In an ABSOLUT World," seemingly turned the world upside down in several images as a way of promoting the brand. This campaign contained yet another example of the advertising world waging war on masculinity. In one ad, the gender roles were completely reversed.

The man was portrayed as being weak, feminine, and shockingly, pregnant. The woman is simply standing there with a drink in her hand.

SPORTS

This chapter began with the story of Bruce Jenner's transition to Caitlyn Jenner and how the sports world, namely *ESPN*, promoted transsexualism. So clearly the sports world does its part to wage cultural warfare on the traditional image of men. Well, the sports world, spearheaded by *ESPN*, also does everything within its power to glorify homosexuality. This is evident by the fact that anytime an athlete comes out as gay, it is always displayed front and center on its website. This agenda was also made abundantly clear in 2014 with the case of Michael Sam.

Michael Sam was a defensive end for the University of Missouri whose stellar play on the field earned him the SEC Defensive Player of the Year Award for 2013. However, he truly made headlines when he came out as gay before the 2014 NFL Draft. This story dominated the headlines with the main question being whether or not this would impact his draft stock. The St. Louis Rams drafted him in the 7th Round. Now for those of you unfamiliar with how drafts in professional sports go, once you get past the 1st Round, there's really no coverage. Draftees get a phone call and that's about it. So you would never expect coverage of a 7th Round pick, right? Wrong. *ESPN* broadcasted the whole thing live. They made sure to capture the exact moment when he celebrated by kissing his boyfriend so everyone could see. Later that summer, *ESPN* would go on to give him the Arthur Ashe Courage Award, one year before they would give it to Bruce "Caitlyn" Jenner.

"THE USEFUL IDIOTS"

I'd like to end this chapter by referencing a term coined by Dr. Anthony Napoleon in his book, *Shadow Men*. Just who are the "useful idiots?" They are everyone given press by the mainstream media. Every individual, organization, and corporation you see promoting an agenda is a useful idiot. The celebrities you follow on social media are useful idiots. They all take orders from the *shadow oligarchs* who are waging cultural warfare on the masses.

Hollywood's celebrities are the most useful idiots of all because everything they do and say defines the culture. In CIA terms, they are the *established citizens*. They can also be considered the armed propaganda team. The masses worship them and copy everything they do because it's "cool." While individual ideas and messages don't seem like much, when you see them repeated everywhere over a long period of time, cultural influence is guaranteed. And right now, the beta male psyop is winning.

Chapter 5:
THE WEAPONIZATION OF SEX

March 31, 2002 – Israeli troops stormed the town of Ramallah, on the West Bank in Israel's biggest offensive against the Palestinian Authority. Once they had full control of the town, they hijacked three Palestinian television stations of Ramallah and proceeded to broadcast pornography 24/7. They forced Palestinian residents to remain in their homes and watch...[29]

Why would they do this? This seems like an odd way of securing control over a population. Or is it? The impact of Internet pornography is a topic that has garnered more attention in recent years, especially among men's interest websites. This is mainly due to the fact that people, more specifically men, are beginning to wake up and realize the long-term negative impact of masturbation to pornography. Many blogs in the general "manosphere" attempt to help men stop once and for all, but let's be honest, these all fall short because "just don't do it" doesn't work in today's world. Many readers say they quit but they don't. They just lie to save face. But they cannot lie to themselves. You have to scare the willpower into them with stone cold truth...

Pornography has always existed in one form or another. In fact, it's so prevalent today that it's hard to imagine a world without it. It's like the Internet. It's just something that has always been there. As with everything else that is prevalent in the culture that we have gone over thus far, you have to put on your critical thinking cap and question this. Why? Why is pornography so readily available? Why does everyone watch it? If you are addicted to it, why is this the case? Thinking broader, why is modern-day culture so sexualized?

Most would answer that pornography is so readily available for the purposes of entertainment or pleasure. That's the basic answer. Your entertainment is always at the bottom of the pyramid. Higher level thinkers would point to money, as that's always a logical answer. "Hey someone is making money off of it!" That used to be the case. But who the hell pays for pornography today? It's everywhere for free. No, the real answer lies with what transpired in Ramallah in 2002. Sex can be weaponized and therein lies the true purpose of Internet pornography.

Internet pornography is a weapon. It is a weapon of spiritual mass destruction. Long-term pornography consumption robs men of their masculine, fighting spirit. It is also yet another tool for depopulation used by the puppet masters. Pornography or even on a broader scale, the hypersexualization of culture, is perhaps the most flawlessly executed psyop of all time because of its subtlety. In fact, author and founder of *Culture Wars* magazine, E. Michael Jones wrote an entire book chronicling how sex has been used to enslave the masses titled, *Libido Dominandi: Sexual Liberation and Political Control.* This hypersexualization of the West is the personification of the Devil himself. The Devil often comes to you as a friend with a smile on his face. Sex, as it pertains to culture, works the same way. It's hidden under the guise of liberation, but in reality, it's enslavement. For centuries, there has always been a select few individuals who understood that the key to conquering the minds of men was rooted in their passions.

"Men are tyrants, in other words, because they cannot govern desire. Their desires govern them." [30]

Jones' historical account provides a mountain of evidence proving that this pattern of control never deviates. Throughout history, the select individuals who pull all the strings have always themselves been the most morally and sexually corrupt people behind closed doors. Instead, of seeking help or exercising self-control, they simply lead the charge calling for the "liberation" of all. Thus, beginning in Central Europe in the mid-eighteenth century, we have seen a slow but steady movement toward public acceptance of sexual perversion. Therefore, their own enslavement became the enslavement of all...

One figure of particular of interest in the book is a man by the name of Wilhelm Reich, who Jones refers to as the father or "high priest" of the masturbation industry. Starting in Vienna in the 1920s, Reich was one of the figures leading the charge of the Sexual Revolution that began in Europe at the time. He was particularly vocal in advocating for the widespread acceptance of sexual perversion and the practice of masturbation as a way of creating "well-balanced" individuals. But what were his beliefs based off of *really*? It turns out they were based off of many things, none of which had to do with the betterment of society or the individual.

First and foremost, Reich's advocacy was simply a way of validating his own lack of self-control in his own life. According to Jones, Reich had been a compulsive masturbator since the age of 4. As he grew older, he began sexually abusing farm animals and by 15, he was a regular visitor of brothels. He eventually became a psycho-analyst from the *Freudian* school where he used his power and trust to sexually abuse female patients under the guise of "cutting edge" treatment. So it's clear that Reich had no control over his own passions. Second, Reich eventually came to understand the impact of hypersexualization on the masses. During speeches, Reich found that by simply "talking dirty," he could hold the attention of even the most distracted crowd.[31] Ultimately, Reich surmised that sex, in every which way and form, was the ultimate "panacea for society's problems," the new opium of the people.

In one of his stand-up specials, comedian Louis CK joked about how "sex is in everything." It was an interesting bit and one that is very relevant to this discussion. He pointed out how the prevalence of sex in all aspects of the culture led to his compulsive masturbation at seemingly random moments, like when he sees a woman reporting the news. Later in the special, Louis CK jokingly begs for it to stop.

"Just the constant perverted sexual thoughts... I'm so tired of those. It makes me an idiot. It's all day too. You can't have a day. I just want to be a regular person and walk around..."

The audience laughed but this lack of self-control over the passions is an issue all modern-day men deal with behind closed doors. The modern-day minds of both men and women are controlled almost entirely by sex. Sex is not just an act but an entity as well. You see it first thing in the morning when you check all of your social media accounts. You hear it in all the music you listen to you. You see it in all the movies, television, and YouTube videos you watch. Now here's an interesting question to ask yourself... Recently, what is the longest you have gone without thinking about sex?

Many think back to the good old days of when they were young children. Have you ever wanted to go back to simpler times? Why? It turns out sex plays a big part in this. When you are a child, you don't think about sex at all, let alone 24/7. You're not fixated on every move you make and whether or not it will ultimately lead to you attracting the opposite sex. You're too busy learning about the world, eating snacks, and playing with toy dinosaurs. You're too busy *imagining*. Your thoughts are pure. As we get older, we become slaves to our passions. Every thought is related to sex. Every move we make is somehow linked to sex. This is understandable because self-control is difficult to master, especially in a culture that does everything it can to support your failure. The continual sexual perversion of popular culture, coupled with the widespread availability of pornography, will always be a weapon that is used to control you. True liberation it seems, lies with controlling it.

Chapter 6:
PORTRAIT OF THE MODERN MAN

If the modern man is viewed as a business, he is a *shitty* business. His brand is a *shitty* brand. Not only does this man not stack up favorably to the man of generations past, he is by far the *weakest brand* of man that has ever existed. He will only continue to get weaker unless something is done about it.

MIND

The modern man is weak in mind. He is weak in mind because there has never been a real reason to become strong in mind. If he doesn't win or if he doesn't quite make it, no big deal! Everyone is a winner. Maybe someone will have sympathy and just give it to him. Individual challenges became continuous cooperation. Continuous cooperation eliminated the need to think. The modern man doesn't think his way out of the box. He looks for a pillow and a blanket. He is the hamster in the wheel. Day in and day out, he does the same thing because his days are governed by the numbing process.

BODY

The modern man is weak in body. Chemical warfare is the main culprit. Testosterone was replaced with estrogen. However, the modern-day lifestyle is also to blame. Above all, the modern man has weak hands and no grip. This is to be expected. The tools of generations past were replaced with video game controllers. Switches and levers became buttons. Buttons eventually became too inconvenient and were replaced with touch screens.

The modern-day man typically fits three molds: skinny twink, skinny fat, fat ass. All three variations are soft in their own way. The skinny twink can be snapped in half by a strong breeze. The skinny fat man and the fat ass can be summed up in one word, *sloppy*. They are *sloppy* in appearance. They are *sloppy* in lifestyle. The posture of the modern man tells you everything you need to know. *Compression is inevitable* but the modern man is soundly defeated by compression as a result of lifestyle. The majority of his days are spent hunched over a screen. His spine is weak and contorted. He has little to no muscle mass because he does not lift weights. His diet is comprised of processed carbs with a heavy dose of alcohol on the weekends. Most importantly, he does not move. He ages fast.

SPIRIT

Above all, the modern man is defeated. His mind is often developed under the guidance of the defeated. Can you expect anything different? Dragons were reduced to myths and sheep became the new reality. Pride became shame. The modern man is ashamed. He feels shame because his body is weak and *sloppy*. His mind is owned by whatever he numbs it with. He is falling apart by his early twenties. Strength went out of style. Weakness is the new hit record. And you know what? He accepts it. He accepts it because the modern man has no fight left in him. The fighting spirit is no more. Not only does the modern man accept death, he often welcomes it. Anything to escape...

This is the portrait of the modern man,
the last line of defense for civilization.

PART II

OF TYRANTS & TELLERS

Chapter 7:
"CIVILIZATIONS AND THE INDIVIDUAL ARE ONE AND THE SAME."

How do you feel after reading Part I? It's okay you don't have to answer right now. The purpose of Part I was to provide you with an in-depth look into what the masses are starting to notice. There is an all-out war on men and this war has been taking place for some time. Sadly, this war on men has been wildly successful. The modern-day man is weak, helpless, and in many cases, accepting of this newly created role for men. So where do we go from here?

We do what men have always done best. We build. Talking about the war on men and examining all the evidence is useless without a plan of action. We're not going to march. We're not going to protest. You know who attends marches and protests? Professional victims. Professional victims scream and shout for a higher authority to have mercy. This victim mentality has no place in the world *Of Tyrants and Tellers*. As a man, you know that the odds are stacked against you in every way possible. So you have two choices. The first choice is to stop right now and become a professional victim. Keep viewing the world in a negative light and do nothing. Or you can build in silence. Take on the role of a professional builder, a builder of a strong, masculine culture that will guide you for the rest of your life.

If you get anything from this work, I want it to be this. Civilizations and the individual are one and the same. The success of both are dependent upon two things: *infrastructure and culture*. Infrastructure and culture are the two most sacred things in the history of mankind. Think of any successful civilization throughout history. What made them successful? They had infrastructure. They were builders. They built roads. They built great structures, many of which still stand to this day. They were socially structured. They had cultures that they were proud of. Their people were defined by their culture. Now think about why these civilizations ultimately collapsed. The reasons remain the same. Infrastructure and culture. These civilizations ultimately became more chaotic. What's the first thing an invading people do besides attacking a population? The invaders destroy the infrastructure, often times decimating the civilization's most culture defining structures. But even civilizations that are not destroyed by warfare still collapse because of their failure to hold their own infrastructure and culture sacred. Buildings and roads get physically worn down, never to be replaced. Culture oftentimes gets destroyed or significantly watered down by immigration.

The same could be said for the individual. Successful individuals are not chaotic. They are not "lost." They are not haunted by an uncertain culture. They abide by the laws of infrastructure and culture. They follow a system of habits that creates a lifestyle. This lifestyle is conducive to their definition of success and happiness. They have infrastructure. They don't allow negative people or forces into their lives because they understand that everything has the potential to influence them. Thus, they understand and abide by the law of culture. Chaotic individuals are "lost" because they do not have these things. They oftentimes do not have a defined infrastructure in their lives. They are unorganized and consistently sloppy. Order is foreign. You can never tell where or when with them, but you can certainly bank on *sloppy*. They also lack culture, or at least an understanding of culture. There is no filter. Anything and everything influences them. They are oftentimes degenerates.

"He doesn't accept the rules of the society we live in because those rules would have condemned him to a life not suitable to a man like himself, a man of extraordinary force and character." [32]

This quote comes from a scene in *The Godfather*, when Michael Corleone was describing his father, the Don. It's a powerful quote, something that obviously stuck with me. But I believe it's something we can all relate to. The current world, this civilization is dying. A world that wages war on men, a world that vilifies strength and masculinity, is destined to become a land of ghosts. And you know what? They can keep that world. They made their bed. Let them lay in it.

Starting with you, we will build our own world. How, you ask? The same way they destroyed it, with infrastructure and culture. That's what the world *Of Tyrants & Tellers* is, after all. It's the new world for men who won't lie down and die. It's the world all men want deep down. The modern man says he wants: success, money, women, happiness, etc. But deep down, what he wants more than anything is: infrastructure and culture. This is what he needs now more than ever. Those are the building blocks. Those are the true keys that unlock it all.

The remainder of this work will be dedicated to building a concrete system, one with infrastructure and culture. That's the *Of Tyrants & Tellers* system.

START SMALL WITH IDEAS.

Chapter 4 should have taught you just how malleable culture really is. As explained, the destruction of cultures often begins very small with the leakage of ideas into mass consciousness. The construction of culture works the same way. So that's where we will start.

THE *OF TYRANTS & TELLERS* ARMED PROPAGANDA LIST

Both the internal and verbal language we utilize in our daily lives has an immense impact on everything, from our self-image to our physical existence. In other words, how we communicate with ourselves ultimately determines where we end up. If the totality of your thoughts equates to those of a loser, that's where you end up. *Loserville*. If the majority of your thoughts and words are those of a winner, that's where you will one day end up. *The Winner's Circle*.

The words you have used in the past do not matter. The future is the only thing that matters and you are building it right now. The following is a list words and phrases to "leak" into your daily life:

Of Tyrants & Tellers

Masculine

Strong

Imagine

Dominate

Win

Money

The future

High energy

Advantage

Opportunity

Elite

High standards

Fast moves

Magnetic

Testosterone

Pride

Precision

Professionalism

19 words and phrases. It often takes the constant leakage of *only 1* word or phrase to completely destroy a culture, both from a societal and individual standpoint. So 19 is more than plenty to set the wheels in motion for you to build something special. The only question that remains is *how* to use this list. And for that I have three suggestions:

1. THE MORNING/NIGHTTIME INDEX CARD RITUAL

This is fairly simple to carry out. Write each of these words on their own separate index card in red ink. Keep these cards on your nightstand. Look at them first thing in the morning. Look at them right before you go to bed.

2. VISION BOARD

Write down these 19 words and post them wherever is most convenient. Post them on the ceiling above your bed. Post them on your walls. Post them on the refrigerator. Post them in your office. Post them up on your mirror. It's up to you. Just post them somewhere that you are going to see them frequently.

3. "CLOSE YOUR EYES AND DRILL IT INTO YOUR HEAD."

This one is the most "far out" but it definitely works. Here's how it goes. You close your eyes and visualize a word. I recommend focusing on one word at a time. Physically see the word spelled out. Choose any style or font. Let's use masculine as an example. With this word, you would close your eyes and physically see M-A-S-C-U-L-I-N-E spelled out. Now imagine this word starting out big. As it rotates clockwise it gets smaller and smaller, eventually disappearing into the center of your head. It's sounds crazy but it works.

Your words, especially the ones you use towards yourself, are everything. These words will birth new ideas. They are your new mindset. They are the building blocks of your new culture.

Chapter 8:
"EVERYTHING FLOWS FROM HEALTH AND PHYSICAL FITNESS."

One of the biggest lies they ever tell you in school is that you should never judge a book by its cover. It's one of those basic, cookie cutter, hack lines they preach to make everyone feel better. After all, everyone's a winner! But the world doesn't work like this. Everyone is not a winner. Everyone judges a book by its cover. The way you physically look is the first thing people notice. This is how both men and women physically assess your brand and your value. Women look at your physical appearance and immediately decide whether or not you are physically attractive. Men look at your physical appearance and assess your overall standing in society.

Your first impression is an important one, because you are a brand competing in the business of people. It is within these initial moments when people estimate your value. "What is this guy's deal?" "Where does he stand?" These are the questions that people answer for themselves early on. Believe it or not, society is relatively accurate when it comes to filtering men based off of physical appearance alone. And the reason relates to that c-word we all love to use: Confidence.

Confidence will always be in a high demand. Men are always on the look out for how they can get more confident. What's the number one thing women say they find attractive in a man? Confidence. To this day, many men either remain clueless or just don't want face reality on how to become more confident. Should you make more money? Yes. Should you get better clothes? Yes. Anything that will positively impact your personal brand value is going to help you improve your confidence. However, they all take a back seat to the long-term impact of improving your overall health and physical appearance.

IT'S ALL ABOUT PRIDE.

Wouldn't it be great if you woke up every day knowing that you had an advantage? Of course it would, especially if you were reminded of this advantage every morning when you got up and looked at yourself in the mirror. The ultimate advantage that a man can have in this day and age is looking and feeling his best. When you start taking better care of yourself, every aspect of your life improves. You become magnetic. You get more attention from women. Men show you more respect. Most importantly, you have pride.

Men used to have pride. They had a lot of it actually. They were proud of their homes. They were proud of their lawns. They were proud of their cars. They were proud of their appearance. There was a time when men would dress like professionals everywhere they went. Look at any old pictures of Yankee games. The stands are filled with men in suits standing next to their sons. Everything in life was done with a sense of pride and precision. There is no pride today. Homes are hoarding hovels. Lawns are rarely maintained. Cars are littered with coins, receipts, and old fries. Most importantly, there is no pride in appearance. *Professionalism* gave way to sloppiness.

Personal pride starts with how you look. When you look more valuable to society as a whole, your life just gets better. This is how the *shadow oligarchs* won. They sapped man of the greatest source of pride and value he could have, *physical strength and fitness*. Chemically, they made man soft and feminine. Culturally, they made him accept it. They normalized weakness and physical sloppiness. Even today, it's not uncommon to hear men as young as twenty-five joke about "getting old" while they playfully pat their beer gut. Physically weak and unfit men should not feel proud or content with their softness. They should feel a sense of shame and this shame should be used as fuel to take action.

The truth is nothing brings greater pride to a man than knowing that he is *physically strong and fit*. Physically strong, fit men have a sense of pride because they know they can take care of business. Thus, they feel confident amongst other men. They don't view other men as above them. They don't feel threatened. They also have pride in knowing that they can protect their women. This is a reality that physically capable men live with every day.

Everything flows from health and physical fitness. A healthy man is a happy man. A fit man has pride in himself and that pride carries into every other aspect of his life. He stands tall and looks people in the eye. People see him and say: "Now that's a confident man!" A confident man is a magnet for anything he wants. A man whose confidence is rooted in his physical appearance has the ultimate advantage. The world is forever his.

Chapter 9:
THE *OF TYRANTS & TELLERS* WEIGHTLIFTING PROGRAM AKA "BASIC CABLE"

Another Louis CK bit I really liked was the one where he talked about what you get with a basic life. The phrase he used to describe it was "basic cable." I liked the phrase so much that it stuck with me all these years. It's the first thing I thought of when I first began thinking of a weightlifting program I could present to you. Those of you who know me know that I can't stand those cookie cutter questions where people ask for the best exercises or the best routine that they could "do" to get bigger and stronger. Even more so, I can't stand the same re-hashed advice that everyone gives out. You ever wonder why no one gets real results? It's because they are all following the same mainstream advice that doesn't lead to real results.

This chapter is the result of 11+ years of experience in the iron game boiled down to this series of questions I asked myself:

"How would I train a total beginner?"

"If you gave me someone who was soft and weak, what would I do to make him carved out of stone?"

"How would I transform someone from soft, doughboy to lean, mean, killing machine?"

"What are the most effective exercises for someone who is just starting out in the gym?"

"What weightlifting program would I give to a generation of soft, weak boys in order to build them from the ground up?"

What you get is the The *Of Tyrants & Tellers* Weightlifting Program aka "Basic Cable." Above all, what you get is infrastructure. Again, why is this generation physically soft, despite working out more than any other previous generation? Why do they ultimately fail in their journey to become physically fit? It's because they lack infrastructure. They just don't have it. Every gym is packed full of *sloppy* looking individuals who never seem to get anywhere from a physique standpoint. For years and years, they remain in a constant state of stagnation. They go to the gym at the same time every day and train the same way every single day. The problem is that they don't train with purpose according to a set infrastructure. They wander around aimlessly and just "do" what's available. But not you. You will train with purpose according to a system that provides infrastructure.

HOW TO THINK *STRUCTURALLY*

Today, when I reflect on my own beginning in the gym, I have a lot to be grateful for. A lot went "right" for me. I didn't have a clue on what I was doing but I had the necessary ingredients for success. I worked out six, sometimes seven days a week. I stuck with the basics. Instinctively, I knew the importance of high volume and frequency.

I also had a "never give up" killer mentality. I just stuck with it and improved little by little.

However, my beginning was not perfect. And in fact when people ask me about it, I warn them not to do what I did. You see, if I have one regret, or should I say one thing I would do different, it would have to do with infrastructure. In the beginning, my workouts did not have a set infrastructure. The game plan was to just show up six days a week and lift for two hours. This only worked for me because I had been a multi-sport athlete my entire life and I had always loved physical activity. This is not ideal for new trainees, especially those who don't already come from an athletic background, or those who don't like physical activity.

So how do you think structurally and organize your workouts according to a set infrastructure? You break down the body according to body parts. In the bodybuilding community, this is referred to as *split training*. Split training works and it is the fastest way to develop lean body muscle mass. It works because it enables you to specifically train each body part with an adequate amount of volume. Mentally, it provides you with infrastructure where you focus on training that specific body part and then you are done. You can move on to the next one. Those who do not use split training or a very watered down version of it, such as the infamous upper/lower body split, lack all of this. Those without this structure often find themselves struggling to get results because they simply do not hit the muscle with enough volume.

So before you begin, the main thing you need to do is change your thinking. Don't think in terms of *days*. Days are not the ideal unit of measure. Instead, think in terms of *body parts*. At the end of the week, the number of days you go to the gym doesn't really tell you much. "I went to the gym four days this week" leaves a lot of questions. Anything, could have transpired during those days. Did you train legs? How much volume and frequency did you use? More importantly, are you improving in size and strength?

Body parts are your new units of measure. These eleven body parts listed below should be the basis of your workout infrastructure. Your week(s) should be assessed based on your ability to train these body parts. I think we can all agree that no matter what type of body we want, we all ultimately want a well-balanced physique. No one wants to construct a physique with glaring weaknesses or imbalances. So it makes sense that you would want to train the following eleven body parts with adequate volume and frequency:

Chest

Back

Abs

Quads

Hamstrings

Calves

Triceps

Biceps

Forearms/Grip Strength

Shoulders

Traps

Now that we have the basis of our infrastructure, we can go over specific exercise examples for each body part. Each exercise is explained in detail along with my reasoning for choosing it. In my experience, these are the best exercises for muscle fiber recruitment, particularly for beginners. These exercises are accompanied by several pictures.

CHEST

Chest was my initial weak point for two reasons. First, from a structural standpoint, I was very delt dominant, meaning the shoulders had a habit of taking over and doing the majority of the work on pressing movements. To be honest, chest was just a weak body part for me. No one has a perfect body. Everyone has their own structural weaknesses and imbalances. The fun part is building those up to become strengths! Second, I initially followed mainstream advice on building my chest and this advice glorified the flat barbell bench as the holy grail of chest development.

I disagree. I believe the flat barbell bench press is the most widely overrated exercise in existence, especially for beginners. It also causes the most injuries. As a beginner, you have very little mind-muscle connection. This is something that you need to build up as you go along. The flat dumbbell bench press is the best exercise for total muscle fiber recruitment and ultimately, total pec development. This exercise requires more effort on your part because you have to pick up the dumbbells, hoist them up, and stabilize them as you are pressing them. Whereas with the flat barbell bench press, you just have to unrack the weight and press it, which does not require as much stabilization.

This first picture shows the dumbbells in place on the knees.
This is prior to lift off.

In this second picture, the dumbbells are at the bottom of
the lift. Notice how the dumbbells are all the way down.
There's only one way to go from here...

Up! Drive straight up. Lower the weights in a controlled manner, and drive straight up. Now again... and again...

BACK

Back is often thought of in 2 ways: width and thickness. This is a great way to go about structurally building a strong back. A strong back is both wide and thick. For this body part, I have two exercises; one focused on developing width and another focused on developing thickness.

As far as width is concerned, nothing compares to pull-ups. Most trainees will opt for lat pulldowns. That's a great exercise for back width as well. However, many will either go too fast with the pace or too *sloppy* with the form, rendering it useless a lot of the time. The pull up is the superior movement because it's just you and a bar. This movement entails total muscle fiber recruitment of the lats. It also involves recruitment of secondary muscles. Most importantly, it promotes the development of grip and overall hand strength.

For thickness, the most effective exercises are the various types of rows. The rows that come to mind are: barbell rows, dumbbell rows, and T-bar rows. Those are going to pack on the most mass. However, most trainees, even those who have years of experience, mess up the form on these types of rows. It's easy to use momentum and get into the habit of rowing with your hands instead of utilizing your back muscles. I like to think of rows in terms of "leading with the elbows." Your hands are "hooks." The way you actually use your back muscles is by leading with the elbows. Thus, seated cable rows are the ideal rowing movement as it's an easy movement to master and more importantly, it enables you to develop this feel of leading with the elbows.

Here is the beginning of a pull-up. It starts with a dead hang.
You can either let your legs hang straight down or cross
them. There is no momentum involved with this lift.

After the dead hang, you pull yourself up. Feel the lats doing the work. Your hands and arms are not doing the work. Your hands are "hooks" meant to grip the bar. Imagine you are pulling your chest towards the bar.

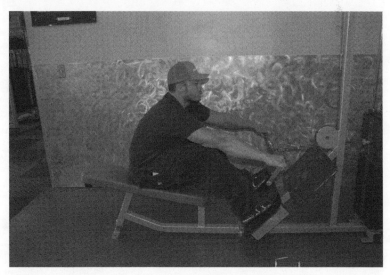

This is the beginning position of the seated cable row where you are grabbing the bar.

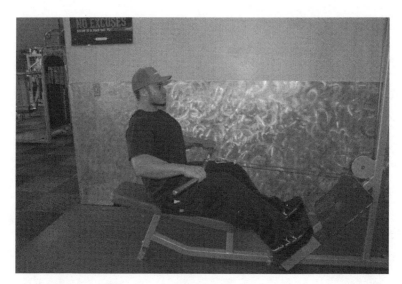

Arch your back slightly. Pull the bar back, leading with the elbows. Feel your entire back, especially the spinal lumbars, contract. Keep going. Keep the form controlled.

ABS

Abs are another one of the glorified body parts that is clouded by myths. In fact, the fitness industry makes billions of dollars a year selling people scams rooted in their desire for abs. You have abs. They are simply covered by a layer of fat. Diet is how you reveal your abs. D-I-E-T. Diet. That's why this program goes great with *The Of Tyrants & Tellers Diet*, which is available for purchase on *Strength By Sonny*.

When it comes to training abs, simple is the key to success. The exercise I chose for this program is hanging leg raises. This is the best exercise, because it works your entire core, forcing you to stabilize. You're also holding onto the bar, so grip and hand strength are also recruited as well.

Like the pull up, start with a dead hang.

Slowly, raise your legs. Feel the movement work your entire core. Slowly, lower your legs and repeat.

QUADS

Squats will always remain king for legs. They are too important to leave out, even in a beginner's program. Squats tax the entire system, not just the legs. Furthermore, the form is not that difficult to master. A beginner just needs to go slow, master the form and not rush to start piling on 45 lb. plates right away.

Load up the bar with your desired weight, resting it on your upper back.

"Squat" down bringing your thighs to parallel (or a little bit further) with the ground. Then drive up. Feel your entire upper legs drive up and contract.

HAMSTRINGS

Many people neglect to train their hamstrings just because it's the back of the upper thighs. They really shouldn't because hamstring training is just as important in creating strong legs as is training the quads. Although leg curls are a great movement for isolating the hamstrings, we are going for efficiency here. Holistically, we are trying to build you into a well-balanced killer carved out of stone. We want lifts that recruit as many muscle fibers as possible.

That's why we are going with deadlifts. However, these aren't your average gym bro "pick it up - drop it down" deadlifts. These are controlled deadlifts. For the grip, we are going with both hands overhand, as this will strengthen your grip, as well as recruit the muscle fibers in your upper forearms. During the lift itself, you're not focusing on your back. You are focusing on your glutes and hamstrings.

The second variation of deadlifts we are going to utilize are dumbbell deadlifts. Dumbbell deadlifts, when done in a controlled manner, offer more individual variation than any other type of deadlift. On top of that, they not only train the hamstrings but also require hand and grip strength throughout the entirety of the movement.

Feet are a little less than shoulder width apart. Hands are in an overhand grip, as opposed to the most common grip where one is overhand and the other is underhand.
The back is straight.

Lower the weight while keeping your back straight. As you squat down, feel your hamstrings and glutes stretching out.

On the lift up, feel your hamstrings and glutes contract. Focus on squeezing the hell out of them!

Start with your back straight and your head slightly tilted up. Dumbbells should be positioned above your quads.

Slowly lower the weights down in a controlled manner. Feel your hamstrings and glutes stretch out at the bottom.

As you lift up, your arms remain stationary. Your hamstrings, and to a lesser extent, your glutes and quads, complete the lift. Feel your hamstrings and glutes contract at the top.

CALVES

Yes, calves are important too. Nothing is more embarrassing than having a developed upper body, developed upper legs, only to have the whole look ruined with stick-like calves. Calves are largely genetic but even if you have weak calves, you can always improve them. Calves respond best to calf raises of all sorts.

The standing calf raise machine is a great movement for hitting the calves with direct resistance. They hit the entire muscle and allow for a full range of motion.

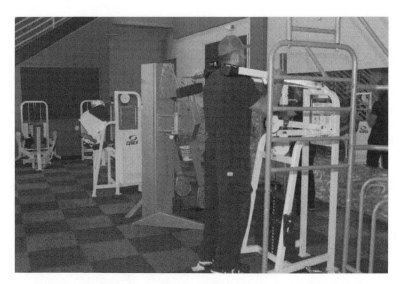

Feel your calves stretch as you lower the
weight all the way down.

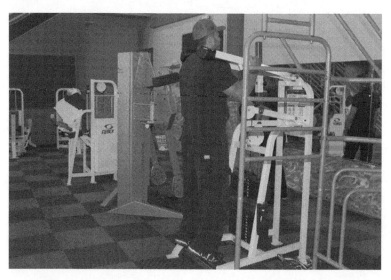

After you lower the weight as low as possible, feel your
calves squeeze and contract as you drive the weight as
high as you can go.

TRICEPS

When it comes to arm training, everyone wants to focus so much on the biceps. However, it is the triceps that make up two-thirds of your upper arm. Therefore, the triceps should receive just as much attention, if not more. Now for the exercise. There's a reason why people love training triceps and it has to do with muscle fiber recruitment and feel. Most tricep exercises are not hard to "feel." To be honest, you can do most of them with relatively loose form and still enjoy the benefits. Thus, narrowing it down to one "best" exercise can be viewed as a challenge. However, one exercise, especially for beginners, stands heads and shoulders above them all, and that is: dips.

Nothing compares to dips, not only as a total mass builder for triceps, but also as an overall developer for the entire upper body. Some go so far as to label dips as "squats for the upper body." I am one of those people. I love dips. Before I ever even touched a weight, I already had a developed upper body and the reason was dips. I had an old treadmill in my room in high school that I never used to run on. Instead, I used it for dips. For me, dips will always be the *king maker* exercise. When I first started going to the gym, my go-to exercise was dips and then eventually, weighted dips. If I could only do one exercise… yup, it would be dips.

Grip the handles and lower your entire body down in a controlled manner.

Using your triceps, drive your entire body up! And then slowly lower yourself down. Repeat.

BICEPS

In addition to chest and abs, biceps are the other "glory" body part that new trainees want to focus the majority of their efforts on. As with triceps, mastering the form on the majority of bicep exercises is not difficult. It just takes time and repetition to develop that feel of the bicep muscle stretching and contracting. Since it takes some time to develop that feel, it doesn't make sense to emphasize isolation movements. Thus, if it's going to take time for you to develop that feel, you might as well use the heaviest, manageable weight and recruit the most muscle fibers. That's why the primary bicep exercise for this program is the barbell curl.

However, I also understand that this movement might not be ideal for some new trainees, especially those who are having trouble breaking the bad habit of momentum lifting and those who are very delt dominant. As a result, I have also included dumbbell curls as an alternative movement.

Load up a straight bar with desired weight. In this picture, I am in the "rest" position. Notice how the arms are NOT locked out. You want to maintain constant tension on the biceps.

Curl the bar upward with your biceps. The upper arms remain stationary. There is no momentum. The part of your body that moves are the forearms which guide the weight up.

This is the stationary (relaxed) position for dumbbell curls.

As with the barbell curl, the upper arm is not moving. The weight is guided up by your hands and forearms.

This is the same movement, curling with the left side. Make sure you use the same weight and volume for each arm!

FOREARMS

Forearms are the number one most neglected body part. Some might say calves but when you think about it, most people are socially aware enough to fear "chicken legs." So they will throw in some calf raises here and there. This isn't the case with forearms. You don't really see people directly training their forearms. They should because forearm training isn't just about building big forearm muscles. Far from it.

Forearm training, or those exercises that directly target the forearms, is really about strengthening your grip and overall hand strength. That's the real prize. We've already established just how soft the modern man is. Well, a big reason for this is his hands. The modern man has soft, weak hands. His grip is also soft and weak. As a result, he is physically weak. His physical work capability is low. The acts of pulling, pressing, and holding go far beyond a few lifts in the gym.

Strong hands and a powerful grip will enable you to improve all of your lifts because they will enable you to do more physical work in general. Strong hands and a powerful grip are an immense source of confidence.

The first exercise we have are hammer curls. Most people ruin this exercise by using too much weight and completing the movement with momentum. Hammer curls, when done properly, are one of the best exercises you can do. Besides working the top of the forearms, hammer curls are one of the few exercises that directly improves your grip and hand strength. They get you in the mindset of "squeezing the life out of the weights." Most people are fixated on improving max deadlifts and bench presses, so what do they do? They do more deadlift and bench press training. In reality, grip strength is often the key to big improvements in lifting capabilities. Strong grip equates to more control over the weight. The more you control a weight or "manhandle it," the easier it is to lift.

The second exercise we have are what I like to call "reverse grip plate raises." These work the top of the forearm and are a great movement to improve both grip and hand strength. You do not need to use heavy plates. In reality, you won't be able to. This movement is so focused and deliberate, 10 lb. plates (or less) is all you need. These will absolutely turn those soft hands into claws of steel!

The third exercise is an old school movement called pin pulls. Pin pulls are essentially the first part of the deadlift or barbell shrugging movement, where you pull the weight from the rack. Since all you are doing is pulling the weight from the rack, this allows you to load up the bar with more weight. This may seem like an ego lift but this is only half true. For one, because you are loading up the bar with a much heavier weight than you are used to, it does a great job of pushing your grip strength to the limit. It forces you to squeeze the life out of the weight. This lift will force those puny wrists and stick like forearms to get thick. Second, because of the weight involved, actually lifting it taxes your entire body. Your entire system is involved in this lift. Third, and this is somewhat related to the ego concerns, pin pulls help you develop that killer mentality where you seek to destroy the weights. It sounds corny, but that killer mentality in the gym is very real. It's often the key difference between results and stagnation.

The fourth exercise is the one arm version of the pin pull. As with any one arm version of an exercise, this is a little bit more difficult, but that's a good thing in the world of fitness. Difficult exercises are often the best ones. In addition to developing grip strength and taxing the entire system, the one arm variation of pin pulls also does an amazing job of helping you develop overall core strength.

This is the beginning or neutral position for hammer curls.
Remember to squeeze the life out of those weights!

Here is a hammer curl with the right hand.

Here is a demonstration of a proper hammer curl done with the left hand. Again, the upper arm is not moving. The upper forearm and to a lesser extent, the bicep, does all the work!

This is the beginning position (bottom) of the reverse grip plate raise movement. Feel the top of the forearms stretch all the way at the bottom.

Lift the plates all the way up nice and slow. Feel the top of your forearms contract. Squeeze the weights as hard as you can! Think of this movement as a "slow flick of the wrist."

This is the beginning part of the two arm pin pull. This is when you establish your grip. Notice the overhand grip as well.

After the beginning position, all you do is "pull" it out of the rack. Squeeze the life out of the weight. Feel it "thickening up" and taxing your entire body. Lower the weight into the rack and repeat.

This is the beginning position of the one arm pin pull. You can put your non-lifting hand on your side or on your hip for stability.

Pull the weight up with one arm, using only your hand as the hook. Squeeze the life out of the weight. Feel it working your core.

SHOULDERS

Shoulder development is key, not only for aesthetic purposes, but also functional ones as well. From an aesthetic standpoint, big powerful shoulders enhance the illusion of overall size. Shoulder width creates a look of dominance and an aura of confidence. From a functional standpoint, strong shoulders or strong "delts" are the basis of pushing strength. If you want to "push" big weight you need strong shoulders.

The first shoulder exercise is standing dumbbell laterals. This is a great go-to movement for shoulders because it creates that illusion of width by capping out the delts. When done with enough volume, this exercise can also be used as a mass builder as well.

The second exercise is an old school exercise known to many as the standing military press. Although the development of shoulder mass is the primary benefit of this exercise, there are in fact, many benefits that come with it. For one, it is an old school power movement that helps increase total muscular development and strength. In fact, Arnold Schwarzenegger himself used to refer to this movement as the "king maker" exercise. This movement enables you to use more weight and physically move that weight a greater distance compared to other lifts. Sadly, this movement is underutilized amongst most trainees.

This is the starting position for standing dumbbell laterals.
Notice how the back is straight and the head is up.

Lift the weights up using your delts. Your arms should
have a slight bend to them. Your hands are hooks
guiding the weight up.

To begin the standing military press, position yourself under the bar. It's better for stability if you have one foot in front of the other. Your grip should be wider than shoulder width.

Starting with your legs, drive the entire weight upward. As you drive upward, position both feet even with one another. Lower the weight and repeat. You can use a little bit more momentum on this movement. Although this will directly hit the shoulders, this can definitely be considered a full body movement.

TRAPS

Trap development gives the physique that complete, powerful look. A man with a weak or non-existent neck looks vulnerable to all sorts of physical danger. A strong, powerful neck and developed upper back signifies unbreakability. New trainees often have the right idea when it comes to trap development because they go for the basics: shrugs.

When it comes to total trap development, nothing comes close to shrugs. So that's the exercise we are going to go with– barbell shrugs. Barbell shrugs enable you to use the most weight so they not only work your entire system, but they also strengthen your hands and overall grip capacity too. When you are doing shrugs, there is no momentum or movement of the neck. Your entire body is stationary. The only part that is moving are your traps.

This movement starts out the same as the two arm pin pull.
The same grip (both hands overhand) is used as well.

With your head positioned down (and eyes up), "shrug" the weight up. The hands are hooks guiding the weight as your traps contract to move the weight.

MISCELLANEOUS/FULL BODY EXERCISE

Kettlebell squats are a movement I wish I had utilized when I was first starting in the gym. This is a full body movement, and with that comes recruitment of a lot of muscle fibers. This movement also gets your heart rate going so it is also a great cardio exercise as well. However, the biggest benefit in my opinion is how this movement forces you to develop that "feel," especially in the glutes, hams, and quads. When done correctly, this exercise enables you to quickly develop that "feel" for these muscles that are doing the work. This is something that took me many years to fully grasp.

Squat deep down. Feel your entire upper legs stretch at the bottom.

Swing the weight upward. Feel your hamstrings and glutes
contract. Lower the weight down and repeat.

This last image shows this exercise when done with both hands.

PUTTING IT ALL TOGETHER

Our goal is simple. We want to strengthen our bodies. We want to become hardened, stone cold killers in a world that has gone soft. We have the structural understanding for that. We know the body parts and we have a guide to the most effective exercises for those body parts. So how do we put it all together?

The *Of Tyrants & Tellers* Weightlifting Program is built upon a foundation of volume and frequency. Each body part is given adequate volume for muscle stimulation and growth. Furthermore, this program also entails frequency. Each body part is trained twice a week. In reality, you actually do this program twice a week. You complete it over the course of three days, take a day off, then go at it the next three days. So you are going to be training six days a week. This is the type of training frequency that will produce the fastest results early on.

As far as volume is concerned, each exercise should be comprised of 4 sets of 20. To limit time spent in the gym, you need to work fast. This means that you should not be resting more than 1 minute in between sets. There's no wandering around and taking your sweet ass time. You're here to get in, work your ass off, and get out. This will keep your heart rate nice and high during the workout. It really is as simple as "the more you put in, the more you get out." Most importantly, for those of you just starting out, you can get away with this type of frequency early on. You have never trained like this, so there is only one way for your body to adapt: build muscle and lose fat. Here is the split broken down by day and body part.

Sunday: Back, Traps, Chest *** end with pin pulls

Monday: Quads, Hamstrings, Calves

**Tuesday: Shoulders, Triceps, Biceps, Forearms
*** end with pin pulls**

Wednesday: Off

Thursday: Back, Traps, Chest *** end with pin pulls

Friday: Quads, Hamstrings, Calves

**Saturday: Shoulders, Triceps, Biceps, Forearms
*** end with pin pulls**

*** Abs should be trained at the beginning of every workout.

Now here are the days fully broken down by exercise for each body part. Remember, each exercise should be comprised of 4 sets of 20 (4*20):

Day 1

Back: Pull-ups; Seated Cable Rows

Traps: Barbell Shrugs

Chest: Flat Dumbbell Bench Press

Pin Pulls: Two Arm Pin Pulls; One Arm Pin Pulls

Day 2

Quads: Barbell Squats

Hamstrings: Barbell Deadlift; Dumbbell Deadlift;
Kettlebell Swing

Calves: Standing Calf Raise Machine

Day 3

Shoulders: Standing Dumbbell Laterals; Standing Military Press

Triceps: Dips

Biceps: Barbell Curl; Dumbbell Curl

Forearms: Hammer Curls; Reverse Grip Plates Raises

Pin Pulls: Two Arm Pin Pulls; One Arm Pin Pulls

FINAL THOUGHTS ON RESULTS AND MINDSET

This program ultimately makes sense because it is built upon the principles of volume, frequency, and speed at which you work. This newfound workload will do wonders for the mind, body, and spirit of the modern man. Think of the sponge that remains dry for a very long time. What happens when you soak it in water? It sucks it all up. That's kind of the same principle we are working with here.

The modern man is essentially a soft, effeminate dough boy. He has little capacity to do physical work with his hands, which is why they are also soft. The modern man is that dry sponge sucking up all that water on this program. This type of workload will force his body to adapt by building lean muscle and shedding body fat.

As far as maximizing your individual results are concerned, this program is simply the beginning of a newfound infrastructure for your own personal health and fitness. The results will come. They always do for those who never give up. Even if you're a hard-gainer, you cannot give up. You must bully your desired results into reality. When it comes to making adjustments to this program, you should always be looking to add more weight in the beginning. You will know when you are ready to do this when you can easily complete 4 sets of 20 for the exercise. Little by little. Step by step. That's how this game is won.

Finally, we come to mindset. As I said, this program is the *beginning* of your journey toward building a strong brand that you can be proud of. The construction of a strong individual begins with a strong, healthy body because a strong, healthy body is the ultimate advantage one can have. Nothing brings a man more confidence than his own physical strength and vitality. This game is about pride. There's no pride in weakness and stagnation. This program is your first step toward building a physical vessel that you can be proud of. Confidence... pride... these are the true pillars of a strong mindset.

Chapter 10:
THIS IS CONOR MCGREGOR'S SECRET TO DOMINATING FIGHTS.

Conor McGregor's rise from poor Irishman collecting welfare checks to UFC superstar and global icon is an amazing story in and of itself. To this day, many answers are floating around as to how Conor McGregor dominates fights. His mindset? His audaciousness? His shit talking? Yes, they have all factored into his success but it is McGregor's relationship with the physical realm itself that enables him to not only win, but oftentimes dominate fights. As you will see, it is the string of events directly before the fight that often indicate McGregor's degree of victory (or defeat) against his opponents.

UFC 189

As McGregor was being introduced, he deliberately stepped to the center of the Octagon and extended his arms to embrace it all. He embraced the ring, his opponent, and the crowd. Although McGregor spent the majority of Rounds 1 and 2 on his back, taking shots to the head, he ultimately dominated the fight by knocking Mendes out in the second round.

UFC 194

This fight was important because not only was it for the feather-weight title belt, the results of this fight forever solidified McGregor as a mainstream celebrity. Again, you knew what the results were going to be right before the fight started. Although Jose Aldo had been the undefeated champ for over a decade, he was visibly tight and compressed. He was taking up as little space as possible. McGregor, on the other hand, was very loose and took up as much space as possible. As McGregor was introduced by Bruce Buffer, he walked out into the center of the ring and completely embraced the physical realm. He would go on to knock Aldo out in 13 seconds.

UFC 196

UFC 196 was the first time Conor McGregor lost in the UFC. When his opponent, Nate Diaz, submitted him in the second round, it shocked everyone. Conor had been on a tear and he still had that aura of invincibility about him. His defeat to Nate Diaz, therefore, humanized him. However, it doesn't appear to be as much of a shock when you take the events leading up to the fight into consideration. Upon entering the Octagon, McGregor was not as loose as he had been in previous fights. He was very tight and did not take up as much space. In fact, if you watch the replay, Diaz was much looser and appeared more comfortable taking up space. Furthermore, when Bruce Buffer introduced McGregor, he did not deliberately walk out into the center and fully embrace the physical realm. Instead, he briefly raised his arms and his movements were very jerky.

UFC 202

The rematch with Diaz was an all-out war that went the distance. It was a close fight by all accounts but no one was really shocked when McGregor was announced the winner by Majority Decision. So what changed? A lot actually, but perhaps the most notable thing to change was McGregor's displayed relationship with the physical realm. It was much better. Prior to entering the ring, he raised his arms in triumph. Upon entering the ring, he broke out into his famous "Conor McGregor walk" or billionaire strut. It was clear that McGregor was more confident in his body and movement this time around.

UFC 205

UFC 205 was the biggest stage for both Conor McGregor and the UFC. Conor was fighting Eddie Alvarez for the lightweight title belt. If he won, he would become the first fighter in UFC history to hold two belts in two different divisions simultaneously. This fight was also taking place at Madison Square Garden in the heart of New York City. That's as big as it gets. Conor completely dominated this fight, dropping Alvarez four times before knocking him out for good in the second round. This fight was also a display of Conor's complete dominance and comfort within the physical realm. He raised his arms in triumph. He did his famous walk. His walk to the center of the Octagon had swagger and he physically made himself as big as possible by totally embracing it all. You just knew he was going to dominate...

So what is the secret to Conor McGregor dominating the fight game? Truly, it can be narrowed down to those moments right before the fight. How he enters the ring. How he walks around. How he moves. How he embraces the crowd. They all factor into his overall confidence in both body and total movement. Conor McGregor is much more attuned to esoteric teachings than most are aware of. He clearly understands the importance of embracing and becoming one with the physical realm.

THE MODERN MAN IS SHRINKING

Shrinkage means the physical phenomena of getting smaller. This is inevitable as you get older. Left up to Mother Nature, you will slowly decay. You will reach a peak height and then slowly lose height as you age. You will reach a peak physique with lean body mass and then you will slowly lose this as well. Thinking beyond chemical warfare, there is absolutely a war on your body. The world is literally compressing you, shrinking you down, and ultimately making you smaller. Maybe you know what I'm talking about?

Chronic stress

All those hours hunched over a desk

All that time hunched over a phone

Lack of exercise or even physical movement

Do you think these factors have zero impact? Of course, they do because strung together, they make up a lifestyle. That lifestyle, the modern-day lifestyle, exacerbates this war of compression on the human body. Not only does this physical shrinkage make you smaller, but it also has an impact on your psyche. No one feels good or confident about themselves when they take up very little space. That's why everyone feels like shit when they fly on an airplane. We are not meant to packed airtight like sardines. Yet many choose to live their lives like this. When life is completely beating you down and compressing you into a diamond, you feel a total lack of control in your life. To be frank, you feel lost. This brings us to the very purpose of this chapter. How do we win this compression war that is constantly being waged on our bodies? More importantly, what are some of the benefits of fighting back via active stretching and movement?

The previous chapter was a great introduction to building a stronger, more confident body that you can truly be proud of. Lifting weights not only makes you bigger and stronger, it also improves your posture and offsets the aging process. However, lifting weights and doing cardio are not the end all be all for physical activity. In fact, it's often the case that they do very little to directly address this compression of the body. Lifting weights forces the muscles to contract. If you do this long enough, without any other activity, you are bound to get stiffer and lose flexibility as you age. Thus, it is imperative that you implement specific stretches and movements that directly fight back against the inevitable shrinking process.

THINK BIG!

The following stretches and movements are focused on one theme: BIG. The idea is to stretch yourself out and make yourself as physically big as possible. All signs point to the modern-day lifestyle doing the opposite. Life beats you down and compresses you until you feel small and helpless. You need to aggressively combat this by opening up and making yourself big. Not only that, you have to think big too!

Start by stretching your entire body up. Go all the way up on your tip toes. Feel your legs stretch. Extend your core all the way up. Use your arms to reach high for the sky.

Now with your feet firmly planted, stretch your body to the left. Keep your arms extended. Feel that stretch on the left side of your core.

Now switch to the right side.

Stretch your entire body upward, extending with your right
hand. Reach as high as possible. Flash the #1 sign.

Now do the same thing with the left hand.

Now extend all the way back. Starting with your feet (on tip toes), extend/arch your legs and back as far back as you can. Keep your arms together and reach back.

This is the same as the previous movement. The only difference is now the arms are not together. Stretch them out in opposite directions as far as you can go. Take it all in and make yourself as big as possible!

Here is the same movement from another angle.

This is similar to what Conor McGregor does when he is introduced. You are embracing the physical realm. Accentuate this movement by going up on your tip toes. Feel your entire body stretch and keep your arms parallel to the ground.

This is the same as the previous movement. The only difference is that you are taking it to another level. Your arms are no longer parallel to the ground. Instead, extend them higher. Make yourself as big as possible.

Now twist your core to the left.

Now twist your core to the right.

Crouch down. Put all of your weight on your left leg. Fully
extend the right leg out. Stretch up with the right arm.
Stretch out with the left arm. Maintain full balance.

Crouch down. Put all of your weight on your right leg. Fully extend the left leg out. Stretch up with the left arm. Stretch out with the right arm. Maintain full balance.

Stabilize your right knee on the ground. Stretch your left leg as far back as possible. Reach for the stars with your right arm. Arch your back. Imagine your right hand grabbing your left foot.

This is the same movement. Opposite arm. Opposite leg.

Claw out with your right hand in a straight line and stretch.
Extend the left leg all the way back in a straight line.

Claw out with your right hand diagonally and stretch. Extend the left leg all the way back diagonally.

Plant both knees on the ground. Claw your arms forward as far as you can go.

Claw out with your left hand in a straight line and stretch.
Extend the right leg all the way back in a straight line.

Claw out with your left hand diagonally and stretch. Extend
the right leg all the way back diagonally.

Sit on your heels. Arch your back. Keep your hands together
and stretch all the way back.

Stretch your entire body upward, starting with your feet on
your tip toes. Spread your arms. Imagine you are a bird ready
for take-off.

Here is the same movement from the side angle.

Stand up and keep your right foot planted. Extend your right arm forward. Extend your left leg back. You core should be about parallel to the ground.

Keep your left foot planted. Extend your left arm forward. Extend your right leg back. You core should be about parallel to the ground.

Extend your entire body upward and raise your arms in victory. You are finished!

HOW TO WIN THE WAR OF COMPRESSION

The stretches and movements we just went over is your *game plan* for fighting back against all the external forces that are shrinking you down and compressing you down into a diamond. Start your morning off by doing these stretches and movements in order. Hold each position for 20 seconds. Make this a part of your daily routine. Watch what happens. When you do, you will enjoy the following benefits:

You will stand tall.

You will have more confidence in your body.

Your movements will be more deliberate and dominant.

Most importantly, you will begin to develop both a better relationship with the physical realm at large and a sense of physical pride in yourself. When most people think of relationships, they tend to only think of relationships with people or with themselves. This is a very one-dimensional way of thinking. One of the most important relationships you are responsible for, is the one with your physical vessel, your body. From there it extends outward to your environment— the physical realm.

Although it is a reality for most, zero physical activity is not an option for you. That's a fast ticket to physical, mental, and spiritual decay. Lifting weights has many benefits. However, lifting weights without any other type of activity makes the body stiff like a board. These types of movements that we just explored are what truly complete your relationship with the physical realm and enhance your well-being. The world is too big for you to spend your days scrunched up in an ever-shrinking ball of nothingness. Be free and spread your wings. Think big. Be big.

Chapter 11:
"MASTER OF SEX"- HOW TO DEFEAT THE PORNOGRAPHY PSYOP ONCE AND FOR ALL

The pornography psyop was successfully carried out just like any other mass scale psyop in the West. It started off with small concessions but when the culture is hit with small "micro" concessions in every direction, that results in big time change. Before you know it, the culture has completely changed, usually for the worse. This is exactly what the *shadow oligarchs* did. Women's clothing slowly became more revealing. Bathing suits became bikinis. Television, movies, and music became more sexually perverse. Female sex symbols slowly got younger. Pornography went from taboo to mainstream. Sex went from the simple act of procreation to a weapon used to enslave the masses.

Sex is everywhere. The widespread use of smartphones and social media have accelerated this enslavement even more. Perhaps that's the best place to start, with your smartphone. Smartphones and sex are very similar in that both are weapons hiding under the guise of liberation. Sexual liberation brainwashed people into believing that rampant, uncontrolled passions was the ultimate form of freedom.

But take a look around. Both sexes are more miserable than ever. Women objectify themselves and sleep with more men than ever. The more sexualized a woman is, meaning the more men she engages in sexual activity with, the emptier she becomes. Women are emotional creatures by nature and are meant to become emotionally attached to a man after sexual intercourse. However, this is not the case today because your average Western woman sleeps around from guy to guy. She is overstimulated and desensitized. Her soul is ultimately lost to *oversexualization*. Men are also overstimulated but in a different way. They overstimulate themselves via pornography consumption and masturbation. The Western man has also lost his soul.

Smartphones promised a very different type of liberation, namely *convenience*. These conveniences became available very gradually. First, it was calling and texting. Then came the camera and Internet access. Before you know it, you had a high-powered machine in your pocket that could do anything instantaneously. These machines enable people to fantasize and completely escape reality, which is why they are glued to them 24/7. Under the guise of convenience, the masses have been completely enslaved. Smartphones took the weaponization of sex to another level. Today, you can get any type of pornography instantaneously on your phone. In fact, this is how most men succumb to total enslavement.

HOW TO KILL 2 BIRDS WITH ONE STONE

Not only are we going to defeat the pornography psyop once and for all, we are also going to significantly reduce your smartphone usage. We will do this with one simple habit. It will be a clean cut. Are you ready?

From here on out, you are to ban all technology from the bedroom.

No television. No computer. No tablet. No smartphone. No nothing. Your bedroom is a sacred place. Unfortunately, most either lose sight of this or never learn it in the first place. In the typical household, this is where men view pornography. They typically view it on their phones and then lay in bed in disgust. From a pure programming standpoint, masturbation to pornography isn't even a matter of making a decision anymore. What tends to happen is you start off browsing around on the Internet or Instagram and you see something that *triggers* you. It's usually a hot chick and because the *shadow oligarchs* have worked overtime to sexualize the culture, they are displayed everywhere. Instagram's algorithms are programmed to promote these types of posts for a reason… Once that happens, you "snap" and before you know it, you're down. You've become the hamster in the wheel.

Now, you don't have that option. There's no trigger and impulse to masturbate because there is no mindless Internet browsing at night. There's no mindless Internet browsing because there is no smartphone. There is no smartphone because there is no technology allowed in the bedroom.

"Either a man imposes self-control on himself by adhering to the moral order, which is reason applied to behavior, or he submits to his passions, which means he submits to control from the outside, either to the passion itself or to the people who exploit the passion for their own benefit, either economic or political." [33]

When you are unable to exert control of yourself, that means someone or something is exerting control over you. Alcohol. Drugs.

Gambling. Sex. These are all vices that destroy the individual and society according to the same template. They are slowly leaked in. Then they are normalized. Then they are in control. As a man, you are born with nature on your side. *Nature designed you to be in control.*

Mastering your sex drive is no easy task because you ultimately *need* it. Perhaps, Jones had a point when he referred to it as "ungovernable." However, I am from the school of thought that the will of the individual can conquer anything, especially when a healthy dose of fear is involved. Fear? Yes, fear. The fear of something bad happening or something good not happening is a powerful form of motivation.

When you are unable to control your sex drive and regularly watch pornography, all you are really doing is bringing pain to the world. You're hurting yourself because you are zapping yourself of your energy and slowly draining your soul. More importantly, you're hurting the world. By regularly hurting yourself, you are preventing yourself from being the very best version of yourself. Thus, you are denying the world from enjoying the fully capable, strongest version of yourself. And if that doesn't work, know this: Every time you resort to pornography, you are breeding *your bloodline* out of existence.

Chapter 12:
THE AGE OF HEROES

What is masculinity? What does it mean to be a man? These are questions that many men today never quite learn the answers to. Many young men have sleepless nights because they are haunted by these questions. In reality, that's all we really want. We just want to find meaning in it all. More than anything, we just want to find our place in the world. It's perfectly understandable. Both men and women are confused now more than ever and no one seems to know why.

But as has been proven, the reason is very simple. The *shadow oligarchs*, the true puppet masters behind the scenes, have turned the world upside down in order to destroy infrastructure and eliminate individual freedom. This quest for total control has required all-out warfare on men. This war on masculinity has largely been won via chemical and cultural means.

So where do we go from here? I guess this relates back to my original purpose in writing *Of Tyrants & Tellers*. Although the roles of men have certainly become blurred in recent years, there's no escaping the history of mankind. First and foremost, men have always been builders. This work represents a call to all men who are unsatisfied with their place in society to start building. You ask questions about masculinity and "manhood." Well, here is your answer.

True masculinity and "manhood" is about achieving the perfect balance of selfishness and selflessness.

That's what the second part of this work is all about. Strengthening your mind, body, and spirit is how you create the very best version of yourself. You're damn right you should be selfish. It's your life, after all. Why wouldn't you customize it and make it as valuable as possible? You are a business. It takes time to build up your personal brand. It takes even more time to master management. Ignore others when they tell you not to be selfish. Selfishness is how you build your brand and master it. Pride, precision, and professionalism is your new code.

However, a selfish individual is an incomplete individual. Selflessness is how you use yourself to better the world. In the end, it's not all about you. The individual is the building block of civilization. You have a greater responsibility to civilization because civilization is what ultimately matters. How are you going to leave a lasting impact and benefit civilization? It starts with you becoming the strongest version of yourself. Now start building it. You absolutely have the power to change the world for the better. This is your story and you are the hero.

ONE SMALL REQUEST

The information contained in this work has the power to get the wheels of civilization spinning in the right direction once again. Most importantly, this information will provide men with the tools of infrastructure and culture that they need to start building a better world. For this work to reach as many people as possible, I need your help!

Please do me a huge favor and write an honest review of this work. The more reviews it gets, the more it will help others in building a mind, body, and spirit that they can be proud of. Thank you very much for reading *Of Tyrants & Tellers*. I look forward to meeting you one day.

ABOUT THE AUTHOR

Sonny Arvado is the creator and founder of Strengthbysonny.com, a website that focuses on a wide variety of men's interest topics. His specialties include: bodybuilding, masculinity, personal brand building, professional networking, culture/psyops, dating advice, social skills, and mindset training. He is available for private consultations. Send him an e-mail at sonny.arvado@gmail.com.

ENDNOTES

1   http://strengthbysonny.com/2017/03/27/
how-to-go-from-stoppable-to-unstoppable-the-secret-power-of-tweaks/

2   Partanen, E., Kujala, T., Naatanen, R., Liitola, A., Sambeth, A., & Huotilainen, M. (2013). Learning-induced neural plasticity of speech processing before birth. *Proceedings of the National Academy of Sciences*, 110(37), 15145-15150.

3   http://strengthbysonny.com/2015/07/16/
the-3-causes-of-a-sexless-youth-and-how-to-potentially-cure-them/

4   http://strengthbysonny.com/2016/11/23/
boiling-frogs-and-tied-up-elephants-this-is-how-you-mold-a-culture/

5   Napoleon, Anthony. *Shadow Men: An Encyclopedia of Mind Control.* College Station, TX: Virtualbookworm.com Publishing., 2015. 4.

6   http://www.history.com/news/a-taste-of-lobster-history

7   http://www.telegraph.co.uk/news/2016/10/01/
us-university-offers-course-for-men-to-deconstruct-toxic-masculi/

8   http://fabfitover40.com/2014/06/06/soy-protein-friend-foe/

9   http://www.huffingtonpost.com/2014/07/15/soy-myths_n_5571272.html

10   http://fluoridealert.org/articles/50-reasons/

11   Yiamouyiannis JA. (1990). "Water fluoridation and tooth decay: Results from the 1986-8^9 national survey of U.S. schoolchildren." *Fluoride* 23(2):55-67.

12   Hao P., Ma X., Cheng X., Ba Y., Zhu J., Cui L. (2010). "Effect of fluoride on human hypothalamus-hypophysis-testis axis hormones." *Pubmed.* 3^9 (1):53-5.

13   http://strengthbysonny.com/2016/12/05/think-like-a-master-what-would-be-your-end-goal-here-are-6-hidden-agendas-of-the-secret-elite/

14   http://thetruthwins.com/archives/30-population-control-quotes-that-show-that-the-elite-truly-believe-that-humans-are-a-plague-upon-the-earth

15   Barzilai, First Roy. The Testosterone Hypothesis: How Hormones Regulate the Life Cycles of Civilzation. Dibrah Publishing, 2015.

16   Napoleon, Anthony. *Shadow Men: An Encyclopedia of Mind Control.* College Station, TX: Virtualbookworm.com Publishing., 2015. 188.

17   http://strengthbysonny.com/2017/05/09/the-fear-economy-is-booming/

18   Napoleon, Anthony. *The Progressive Virus: Why You Can't Permit it to Go Forward.* College Station, TX: Virtualbookworm.com Publishing., 2012.

19   https://www.wsj.com/articles/paul-mchugh-transgender-surgery-isnt-the-solution-1402615120

20   http://strengthbysonny.com/2017/01/03/why-are-the-kardashians-famous/

21   Gabler, Neal. An Empire of Their Own: How the Jews Invented Hollywood. New York: Doubleday, 1988, 7.

22   PSYOP: Military Psychological Operations Manual. Lexington, KY: Mind Control Publishing, 2009. P. 1-2.

23   PSYOP: Military Psychological Operations Manual. Lexington, KY: Mind Control Publishing, 2009. P. 1-5.

24   Nagy, A. M. CIA: Psychological Operations in Guerrilla Warfare. S.p., 2013. P. 7.

25   Nagy, A. M. CIA: Psychological Operations in Guerrilla Warfare. S.p., 2013. P. 11.

26   Nagy, A. M. CIA: Psychological Operations in Guerrilla Warfare. S.p., 2013. Appendix.

27   Nagy, A. M. CIA: Psychological Operations in Guerrilla Warfare. S.p., 2013. P. 52.

28   http://www.independent.co.uk/arts-entertainment/films/news/ michael-douglas-social-media-obsession-is-to-blame-for-crisis-in-young-american-actors-10372920.html

29   http://www.news24.com/xArchive/Archive/ Porn-the-new-weapon-of-choice-20020330

30   Jones, E. Michael. Libido Dominandi: Sexual Liberation and Political Control. South Bend, IN: St. Augustines Press, 2005. P. 28.

31   Jones, E. Michael. Libido Dominandi: Sexual Liberation and Political Control. South Bend, IN: St. Augustines Press, 2005. P. 253.

32   Puzo, Mario. *The Godfather*. New York: Berkley, 2016. P. 349.

33   Jones, E. Michael. Libido Dominandi: Sexual Liberation and Political Control. South Bend, IN: St. Augustines Press, 2005. P. 266.

Made in the USA
Middletown, DE
09 November 2021